BRIDGING THE GEN

How to Get Radio Babies, Boomers, Gen Xers, and Gen Yers to Work Together and Achieve More

Linda Gravett, Ph.D., SPHR and
Robin Throckmorton, M.A., SPHR

CAREER
PRESS
Franklin Lakes, NJ

BRIDGING THE GENERATION GAP
Edited and Typeset by Kara Reynolds
Cover design by Jeff Piasky
Printed in the U.S.A. by Book-mart Press

To order this title, please call toll-free 1-800-CAREER-1 (NJ and Canada: 201-848-0310) to order using VISA or MasterCard, or for further information on books from Career Press.

The Career Press, Inc., 3 Tice Road, PO Box 687,
Franklin Lakes, NJ 07417
www.careerpress.com

Library of Congress Cataloging-in-Publication Data

Gravett, Linda.
    Bridging the generation gap : how to get radio babies, boomers, Gen Xers, and Gen Yers to work together and achieve more / by Linda Gravett and Robin Throckmorton.
        p. cm.
    Includes bibliographical references and index.
    ISBN-13: 978-1-56414-898-8
    ISBN-10: 1-56414-898-X
        1. Work. 2. Conflict of generations. 3. Psychology, Industrial. I. Throckmorton, Robin. II. Title.
HD4901.G756 2006
658.3'145--dc22

2006011950

Dedication

We would like to dedicate this book to our families, long-suffering in their willingness to proofread, serve as a sounding board, and live without our company for days on end while we were writing. We couldn't have done this without you.

Acknowledgments

We'd like to acknowledge the 2,500 people across generations who patiently filled out a survey or sat through an interview as we barraged them with questions about their life, their dreams, and their needs and wants in the workplace. You're anonymous to readers of this book in name, but many will relate to your comments!

Contents

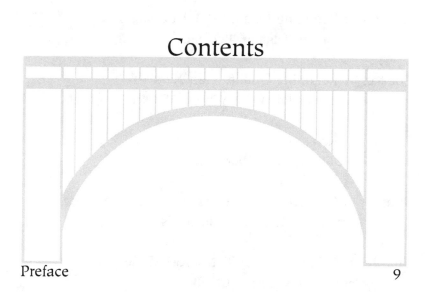

Preface

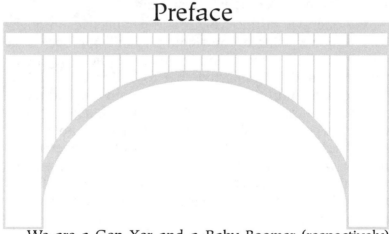

We are a Gen Xer and a Baby Boomer (respectively) who have successfully worked together in several capacities over the years. We know it's possible to come from different perspectives and collaborate to achieve mutually satisfying results. Our experiences together and observation of people in the workplace compelled us to write this book about ways to recruit, develop, and retain workers across all four generations in today's workplace.

This book demonstrates how members of any generation can relate to people they work with in other age groups to minimize conflict, miscommunication, and wasted energy. Our hope is to assist managers in their efforts to maximize the talents and energies of the entire workforce. We've included true scenarios and case studies along with our own recommendations for effective ways to handle each situation.

Our book is heavily researched with one-on-one interviews conducted over a five-year period, from 2000 to 2004. Coauthor Linda Gravett interviewed 500 individuals in each of the four generations in today's workforce: Radio Babies, Baby Boomers, Gen Xers, and Gen Ys. We are constantly adding to our research and plan to publish ongoing articles on our findings over the next few years.

We offer two distinct voices and perspectives throughout the book, using a point-counterpoint approach that surfaces both differences and similarities across generations. We model coming together to bridge communication gaps to minimize unnecessary and unproductive conflict, to show that it is possible and profitable. We will also share generational pet peeves gleaned from our interviews about working with members of other generations, and we will endeavor to debunk commonly held stereotypes about each generation in order to help you find—and retain—the best and brightest of *all* generations.

Chapter 1

Why Can't We All Just Get Along?!

Linda Gravett:

Does this sound familiar?

The sales manager, a man about 50 years old, is at the front of the room. He's addressing sales reps of varying ages who have flown in for the annual meeting. As the sales manager is explaining next year's goals and exhorting everyone to "pull together" to achieve targets, a group at a table in the back is clearly disengaged. There's a lot of eye rolling and pretend gagging from this group of 25-to-30-year-olds.

What's going on?

I've observed this scenario—or versions of it—frequently over the past few years: Older, experienced staff tries to guide and lead the "young pups." That guidance, though well intentioned, isn't always well received.

As a consultant called upon to help this sales department work together more effectively with less conflict, I sat in on sales meetings for the company for a few months. In private, I asked younger sales reps why the sales manager turned them off. They said, "He just gives us the rah-rah cheerleader bit. Just tell us our goals and get out of our way. I'm in this for me, not the so-called team."

In private, I asked the sales manager how he perceived his sales reps. He said, "The kids have no sense of tradition or respect. They have no work ethic."

Scenarios similar to this one are being repeated in organizations around the country. Miscommunication and conflict across generations affects productivity, morale, and customer satisfaction. So we must do better if we want our organizations to survive and thrive.

We operate in a competitive global economy in which technology moves at warp speed and customers are diverse in terms of culture and language. To be successful, our organizations must harness the energies and talents of *every* employee, regardless of age.

Robin Throckmorton:

Successfully harnessing the energies and talents of *every* employee regardless of age is a challenge for all of us, but is truly beneficial if it can be accomplished. It can only be accomplished if we build a bridge between the generations to help them more effectively collaborate and communicate.

Let me share with you one of my coaching assignments:

The manager was in her late 40s to early 50s, managing a man in his mid-20s. As she put it, he was a "young pup" with the energy and ambition of a toddler. Most of the other employees were 10–30 years older than him as well. Needless to say, there was a definite clash between the generations.

The "young pup" was eager and ambitious to learn and do as much as he could. And he expected credit for his accomplishments. On the other hand, the others had put in their time and did not like being shown up or having "the way it had always been done" challenged.

This friction is common when people from various generations work together. But if you can't get everyone to work together, the employees, the organization, and the customers all suffer from this generational divide.

In this situation, I was able to meet with the manager and the employee separately and then together to help them understand the differences between their generations. Together, we brainstormed ways to use these differences as advantages in their respective roles and to the organization. For example, helping the manager see that the "young pup's" ideas may be new and better than anything tried before, and helping the employee listen and learn from the manager and other coworkers what has been tried and why it did or didn't succeed. By doing this, they may be able to combine both fresh and tried ideas to create an even better way of doing things. Soon after they began implementing their combined ideas, the friction lessened and they were able to spread the ability to work with others of differing generations throughout the organization.

Linda and Robin:

In this book we offer concrete suggestions for narrowing the divide between generations. There are four generations attempting to work harmoniously in today's workplace, and disparate perceptions, worldviews, experiences, and communication styles sometimes block the synergy required for organizations to succeed. Our thoughts on how to address these generational barriers are based on research as well as our own experiences and perceptions gained through growing up in our respective generations. We come from different generations (Linda is a Baby Boomer and Robin is a Gen Xer), yet we've found we can work together as colleagues—and friends—by leveraging two factors: our common values and mutual respect.

Research for the book

Between January 2000 and December 2002, Linda interviewed 500 people in each of these four age groups:

58–73

39–57

27–38

15–26

She also conducted follow-up interviews in late 2004 and early 2005. Every person interviewed was asked these six questions:

1. What factors affect your happiness in general?

2. What entices you (or would entice you) to join an organization?
3. What compels you to stay with an organization?
4. What factors shaped your perspectives when you were growing up?
5. What characteristics of other generations in the workplace bother you the most?
6. What do you want other generations to know about you and your generation?

The responses were candid, often unexpected, and always enlightening! Throughout the book we'll share these different outlooks and comment on them through the lens of our own unique perspectives.

The players in today's workplace

Depending on which author you read, there are many different yardsticks for the birth years of the five generations we'll discuss in this book. Most sociologists suggest the following breakdown, and this is the one we'll be using for our purposes of discussion:

Radio Babies (or Silent Generation): born 1930–1945

Baby Boomers: born 1946–1964

Generation Xers (or Baby Busters): born 1965–1976

Generation Ys (or Generation Why): born 1977–1990

Millennials: born 1991 or later

For the most part, we will be discussing the four current generations in the workforce, because the Millennials don't join us until 2007 when the oldest turn 16. However, we have included a chapter on this generation (Chapter 9) to help you prepare for them.

Of the key generations in the current workplace, Generation Y (80 million strong) is the largest group, followed by Baby Boomers (78 million), the Silent Generation (63 million), and Generation X (48 million) according to the Bureau of Labor Statistics (Dohm 2000). Information from the Census Bureau tells us that the 25–54-year-old demographic group is growing at only a 1.2 percent rate, whereas the 55–64 year olds are growing at a rate of 47 percent. Clearly, the labor force is getting older at a faster rate than they can be replaced, so keeping older workers longer and preparing younger workers for succession sooner is critically important in the global marketplace.

In this book, we will endeavor to shed some light on new ways that organizations can recruit, manage, motivate, and retain a workforce that spans all five generations.

Summary

Miscommunication and conflict across generations can cost your company thousands of dollars in lost revenue and employee turnover. In this global marketplace, the skills and talents of every single employee are valuable. The key to harnessing the talents of each individual is clarifying common goals and objectives and guiding employees through the organization's mission and vision.

Case Study: Managing Gen Ys

The coffee shop is humming with activity, as is always the case around 9 a.m. Sue, the manager, is focused for the moment on a problem employee. She'd rather concentrate on setting up for the lunch crowd, but her young waitstaff always seem to be vying for her attention.

Sue's current "problem" employee is Mike. He isn't really a bad employee; in fact, he seems pretty average: 19, working while in college, doing a pretty good job most days. Sue worked some similar jobs herself, working 35 hours a week in a restaurant while she was a full-time student. She smiled as she reminded herself that she kept a 3.8 G.P.A. She hadn't needed or expected a lot of "attaboys" when she was younger. It's a good thing, too, because she didn't receive constant praise—just a steady paycheck.

This kid, Mike, has pulled her aside for the fifth time this shift to verify that he's handling a task well and get her to praise him in front of coworkers. Mike seems to crave constant attention and recognition, even for just showing up on time or busing a coworker's table occasionally. Other employees Mike's age seem to be the same. They're always asking, "This is a great way to do this, right?" You'd think they invented service with a smile, and just for adequate service they believe a raise is in order.

Questions for Discussion

1. What generational mindsets may be in operation in this scenario?

2. How can Sue provide the recognition her young employees seem to want in ways that don't drain her time and energy?

Solution

The coffee shop's young employees tend to have a Gen Y's sense of entitlement...to constant feedback, recognition, and attention. The manager "paid her dues" and has a difficult time understanding this younger generation's seeming craving for nonstop attention.

Sue could call an employee meeting just before a shift or during a slow time and brainstorm ideas for recognition. The employees would then generate suggestions that are appealing to them, so Sue doesn't have to guess. It's very likely that the incentives they come up with would be inexpensive—such as a 20-minute break for a week rather than a 15-minute break. As cheesy as it sounds, Sue could consider having a bell that is rung loudly whenever an employee gets a customer compliment or helps out a coworker. Let the customer or coworker be the bell-ringer. For Sue, when she does give kudos, they must be sincere. A Gen Y can spot a phony a mile away and is completely disenchanted with a boss who doesn't provide sincere feedback.

Chapter 2

Let's Talk Dollars and Sense

Linda and Robin:

You may be thinking, "So why should I care about the generations in my workplace—how does this issue affect my department or company's profitability?" It's a fair question, and we're going to address it in this chapter.

Unemployment steadily declined in the United States in 2005. The Bureau of Labor Statistics reported that unemployment in November 2005 was 5 percent, and Lawrence Kudlow predicted at the end of that year that in 2006 the economy would produce jobs at a steady pace, the stock market would be healthy, and gasoline prices would continuing their downward trend (Kudlow 2005).

Historically, when unemployment rates drop, more workers are tempted to "test the waters" and look for jobs elsewhere. This is particularly true if they're disenchanted with their current workplace. Do you think this can't be true in your organization? According to the November 2005 Spherion Employment Report, "nearly 40 percent of the working adults in the U.S. said they are likely to look for a new job in the next 12 months" (Spherion 2005). What would happen if even half this number of employees left your organization? Would it impact your productivity? Customer service? Profitability?

Another key projection comes from the U.S. Bureau of Labor Statistics: By 2010 the United States will be short 10 million workers—this is actually 10 million workers *with the right skills*. Remember in the late '90s when we were willing to fill an empty chair with any warm body at any cost? At that time, we were only short 3–4 million workers. There simply aren't as many Gen Xers (born 1965–1976) as retiring Baby Boomers (born 1946–1964). The math should tell us that we have to plan for recruiting—and keeping fully engaged—the people with the skills, knowledge, and competencies our organizations need to survive and thrive. And we have to be willing to do things a little differently. Are we willing to hire a retiree part-time with a flexible schedule and offer him or her benefits? It may be necessary if we want to get an employee with the skills we need. You will have to be creative if your organization is going to survive the labor shortage.

We mention retention as an important factor in this chapter for one key reason: Turnover is much too costly for any of our organizations to deal with! Depending on whether you're replacing a non-skilled, semi-skilled, or professional-level employee, turnover costs could range from 50 to 150 percent of the departing employee's annual wage. To clarify, if you're paying a salaried employee $50,000 a year, direct and indirect costs for finding, selecting, and training a replacement employee could be as high as $75,000. In Appendix B you'll find a worksheet that you can use to help itemize your direct costs of turnover.

In light of statistics such as that, one would think that most organizations would conduct internal studies on the demographics of their workforce to assess what steps should be taken to ensure there is adequate "bench strength" for projected retirements. Quite the contrary! According to a Conference Board report, 66 percent of companies have not conducted an age profile of their organization and don't have hard data on how upcoming retirements will affect their operation (Muson 2003). In Figure 2-1 on page 24, we've provided you with a list of actions you can begin taking immediately to help your organization improve its retention.

One in four of the Baby Boomers we interviewed is thinking about retirement. Their companies should be thinking about how to replace them with high-quality employees—or better yet, entice them into semi-retirement to be able to continue to benefit from their skills and knowledge while they mentor and teach others. Our youngest generation, Gen Y, thirsts for this kind of knowledge and in return is willing to help the older generations with the rapid changes in technology. We as organizations just need to help bridge the gaps between the two.

Development and retention of quality employees is an important concern for organizations today, and retention of valued customers and colleagues is also critical. Consider the following true scenario.

A 60-year-old CEO of a small but highly profitable company walked into a start-up high-tech organization one morning. He was interested in becoming a venture capitalist (someone who provides financial backing for start-ups in return for a percentage of profits) as an investment and for the fun of helping out younger entrepreneurs. He had not called ahead but thought he'd take a chance on finding the company's CEO or CFO in and available for a few minutes. The receptionist ignored him to finish a personal phone conversation that took five minutes. She inquired whether he had an appointment when he asked to meet with the CEO or CFO about long-term planning for the company's financial future. When she called the CEO, she said (within earshot), "There's an older guy in the lobby who wants to discuss financial planning with you." The CEO did come out to the lobby and met the potential venture capitalist, who was temporarily on a cane because of a skiing accident. The younger CEO immediately dismissed the other's viability as a long-term investor and not-so-politely cut the conversation short. Three weeks later, the senior CEO found another young company in which to invest. About 18 months later, his "adopted" company went public. The first company he visited went out of business.

Here's another true scenario.

A 45-year-old sales rep for a manufacturing company visited a 20-something purchasing manager with a potential client company. The meeting was simply a courtesy call so the sales rep could introduce herself and start to build a relationship. As the purchasing manager walked into the lobby, the sales rep couldn't disguise quickly enough the look of unhappy surprise on her face because the young man was, well, so young. During their brief meeting, the sales rep tried to impress upon the purchasing manager how her experience and expertise could help him purchase the right equipment for his company. She offered to coach him through dealing with the company's CFO so he could purchase the equipment he felt was needed. As she left, she said, "I'm glad to do all I can to help you kids out." She didn't get the account. The $650,000 yearly account went to a competitor, and the sales rep has no clue how that could have happened.

From scenarios such as these, which we witness on a regular basis, it's becoming clear that companies are losing money and opportunities because of misperceptions and misunderstandings about other generations in the workplace. We want to make sure this doesn't happen to *your* company. Read the rest of this book for a better understanding of generations in the workplace and lots of strategies you can use to help bridge the generation gap.

Summary

Check your budget. Typically you'll find that the largest line item is payroll. Why? Because your people are a key resource to making your company successful. Therefore, it only makes common sense (and bottom-line cents) to ensure you understand your employees and do what you can to retain and develop their skills to avoid or minimize the costs of conflicts and turnover. To begin understanding your workforce, conduct an evaluation of the ages of your employees and how the breakdown of the ages could impact your long-term staffing needs as well as interim internal relations with employees.

Figure 2-1: Retention: What can I do?

Evaluate the ages of your workforce. Do you have a problem on the horizon?

Develop strategies for attracting and retaining the retiring workforce. Just because an individual wants to or is ready to retire doesn't mean you can't create a mutually beneficial opportunity (such as part-time or flexible hours with benefits).

Identify ways to be more efficient. How can you increase productivity without increasing staff and putting more work on the current staff's shoulders (for example, reduce the number of steps in a process, reduce space, and optimize technology)?

Create a formal process to assess manpower planning over the next five–10 years. What skills will you need? How can you prepare to have the staffing resources to meet those needs either through in-house training or external recruiting?

Evaluate current turnover. Why do employees leave your organization? Are there themes emerging showing certain types of positions and/or age groups that are turning over faster than others? What is it costing you? What can you do to decrease turnover?

Establish an open two-way communication on all issues. Is your organization perceived as very open with employees? Do employees feel you freely share information about the organization with them, or do they read about it in the paper?

Assess skill development commitments. What are you doing to develop the skills of your current employees? Is it adequate? What are you doing to prepare your future workforce?

Proactively work to retain talent. What are you doing to retain your "A" players? "B" players? What are you doing to improve or release your "C" players?

Case Study: The Cost of Miscommunication Across Generations

Susan, a 22-year-old business analyst with We're the Top Consulting, is sitting in front of the VP of human resources for the third time since she accepted the position four months ago. When Susan started with the company, she was fresh out of Harvard and eager to share what she learned both in the classroom and in internships with other national consulting firms. The person sitting in front of the human resources professional was bewildered and disillusioned.

Susan came to human resources for the first time after only three weeks in her position. She had just had a confrontation with a colleague who had "yelled at her" in the lunchroom because she wasn't ready to leave the office to sit in on a client meeting. Susan was baffled by her coworker's need to leave "right now" to get through traffic. She was only five or 10 minutes away from finishing her lunch, and surely having a healthy meal was important to get her through the rest of the day. Susan was so upset over this confrontation that she opted out of going to the client meeting and was unable to concentrate for the remainder of the afternoon.

During that first meeting with HR, Susan was asked whether the coworker actually raised his voice or said anything that was disrespectful. Susan responded that it wasn't so much the volume as the tone of the conversation. She said that she was not accustomed to being spoken to in that manner and she didn't know how to respond. The HR representative spent an hour with Susan during that first meeting, trying to coach her on ways to deal effectively with assertive coworkers.

Susan came to human resources for the second time after having what she called a "fight" with her supervisor, a 12-year veteran of the company who has mentored several new employees over the years. Susan complained that her boss was insisting that she submit a draft of her reports to him prior to sending the reports on to her clients. Susan was of the belief that she had sufficient experience and education to send reports out on behalf of the company without having them second-guessed by anyone else. The human resources representative spent an hour meeting with Susan's boss to determine his perspective.

Although he thought Susan's work was quite good, his practice has been to at least glance over new analysts' reports in their first few months to be certain they reflected the policies and philosophy of the organization.

The HR representative spent a second hour meeting with Susan and her manager together in order to discuss an appropriate way for them to ensure that Susan's need for autonomy and the boss's need for accuracy were both met.

Now, Susan believes she's involved in a crisis situation that requires the attention of the top human resources person. Although it's only March, she has advised her manager and coworkers that she will be taking the month of September off in order to accept her parents' offer to take her with them to Europe for vacation. Susan believes this is the chance of a lifetime that may never come again. Her manager and coworkers believe she should follow the company's policy that provides one week of paid vacation after one year. Also, September is "crunch time" for Susan's department and none of her colleagues are planning to take any time off that month, paid or unpaid. She believes they are pressuring her too assertively to forego taking a month off and that the entire "one week after one year" policy should be revisited by the company. She wants a decision today so that she can advise her parents whether they should purchase a ticket for her.

Susan reiterated her major concern to the VP of human resources: Her manager and coworkers are mean to her and disrespectful of the value she brings to the organization.

Questions for Discussion

1. What do you think the misunderstandings and discussions with Susan have cost the organization up to this point?

2. If you were the VP of human resources, how would you handle this situation?

Solution

The primary cost to the organization is opportunity cost—the money a company spends on one activity at the expense of another (usually better) opportunity. In this case, the cost is lost time for Susan, her manager, and the human resources staff. Even though these employees are "on the clock" anyway, think about the more productive and profit-generating activities they could be engaged in, rather than taking time to discuss misunderstandings. Susan lost four hours of productive time after she had her first disagreement over finishing her lunch quickly to get to a client meeting. Her coworker had to take extra time to bring her up to date about the client discussion. Additionally, there's the cost of Susan's time and the HR representative's time to handle the first complaint. Count in the cost of Susan's time with the HR person for the second issue, as well as the HR rep's time and the manager's time to resolve the problem. When you consider the cost-per-hour of the employees' time, hundreds of dollars in opportunity cost have been spent.

Susan has the perception that her managers and coworkers are too hard-driving and focused on their work. She believes they're pressuring her to be as ambitious as they are and to sacrifice her well-being and family time for the company. Susan's manager and coworkers view her as a valuable asset to their department—when she turns her time and attention to the work at hand. They're apprehensive that her first priority is not her job and that they will have to pick up the slack caused by her lack of commitment.

We suggest that the VP of human resources communicate to Susan the mission, vision, and core values of the organization, as well as Susan's role in achieving business objectives. Susan may be unclear about how and why she supports key objectives and consequently doesn't have the same sense of immediacy with projects as do her colleagues. The VP of human resources should also coach Susan's manager about ways to be specific and concrete about *why* Susan is undertaking each assignment, as well as the short- and long-term impact on clients. As to the request for a month off, the negative impact on the company appears to outweigh the need to acquiesce to Susan's request. We would clearly explain the business need for her to be at work during the month of September, realizing that she may decide to resign her position or select a different month for the trip.

Chapter 3

The Generations in Context:
How Did We Get This Way?

Linda:

I was in Mr. Boylan's 8th-grade American History class that cold, gray day in November 1963 when the school principal made the announcement over the speaker system: President John F. Kennedy had been assassinated in Dallas, Texas. Along with many of my classmates, I lost trust that day. My world would never be the same.

Robin:

I grew up watching my parents struggling to run a 40-year-old family-owned retail business. For years, the business was extremely successful, growing to more than seven stores. But through my early teenage years, I watched the local factories lay off or transfer workers who had been with them their entire lives. This loss of jobs forced both parents in many families to work, and resulted in stress that led to many divorces and dysfunctional families. I was determined that my world would not be like this when I grew up. I didn't trust large companies and I wouldn't put all my eggs in one basket.

Linda and Robin:

As we were growing up, we were uniquely influenced by our parents, teachers, friends, media, and world events. But Morris Massey, who wrote *The People Puzzle*, suggests that we share a history and common experiences with other members of our generation, and that shapes our collective worldview. That is not to say that all people born in the United States in the 1960s, for example, are completely alike in their thinking. Far from it. There are, however, many experiences that this group shares, so they can relate on some level to one another.

In this chapter, we'll place the four generations in today's workplace in context. For each generation we'll highlight important world events and social mores that were most influential. Our intent is to shed light on why people might say or do things that seem inexplicable to members of other generations.

Linda:

When I was traveling around the country interviewing members of the workforce, I was struck by an inescapable phenomenon. Whether male or female, African -American or Caucasian, Midwesterner or Southerner, some events that took place in the world had significant and similar impact on people when they were young. I'm going to address some of those events that had an affect on Radio Babies and Baby Boomers, and Robin will highlight events that affected Generations X and Y growing up.

Radio Babies

You know you are a Radio Baby if...

- ❑ You remember how to entertain yourself when there's no TV.
- ❑ You remember when TV was all black and white.
- ❑ You can stretch a buck nine ways to Sunday (and you understand that phrase).
- ❑ You use a computer but you're still afraid you'll break it.
- ❑ You remember *doing* ballroom dancing instead of watching it on TV.
- ❑ You ever mowed a yard with a push mower (not motorized).
- ❑ One of your first cars had running-boards on it.
- ❑ You listened to Ricky Nelson on the radio.

Some comments from the Radio Babies we interviewed were:

I'd be happy to share some of the wisdom it's taken me years to accumulate. But nobody asks me!

Believe it or not, I can still think, talk intelligently, and wiggle all my toes.

I'd stay in the workplace another 10 years if I could find a company that's willing to be just a little flexible about start times. I'd like to read the paper over coffee at Starbucks before I come to work.

The mind still works, I'm still creative, and I care about the quality of my work.

I may remember WWII, but there's still enough room in my head to learn the latest technology.

I can do more than share stories about the good old days. I can help shape the future.

I don't need help crossing the street, remembering numbers, or finding the conference room.

Don't hesitate to check ALL my references from past employers. PLEASE do check so you know what I bring to the table.

Radio Babies: A profile

Radio Babies were born between 1930 and 1945. Sociologists have dubbed this generation with this name because radios were a staple in many American homes when this generation was growing up, and TV was yet to come.

When Radio Babies were young, they had heroes to look up to and admire. President Truman made it a goal to unite Europe under American leadership. Astronauts John Glenn and Neil Armstrong traveled in space. Big Band leader Benny Goodman emerged from a childhood of poverty to make a tremendous impact on the music industry. Cassius Clay "floated like a butterfly and stung like a bee" to become a boxing champion in the 1960s. Baseball great Jackie Robinson carved a path for African-American athletes and was an idol to many.

Some of the oldest Radio Babies fought in World War II, and some of the younger members of this generation fought in the Korean War. The enemy was clear: communism. The cause was just: keeping the world free of communism. The soldiers who came home from these wars came home as heroes and helped develop a time of relative prosperity in the United States. During WWII, those left at home were rationing goods, pulling together, and making sacrifices for the good of the country.

The former Soviet Union launched Sputnik I in 1957. This event marked the beginning of the space age and exciting by-products and inventions, such as microwave ovens and frozen foods, which changed how people lived. Just as generations to come, Radio Babies would witness rapid and marvelous techno-logical changes.

Authors such as Claire Raines (*Generations at Work*) have described Radio Babies as conservative, fiscally prudent, and loyal to their employers. My mother is a member of this generation, and these attributes certainly describe her. We were shopping recently and she noticed a package of dust cloths on the shelf that cost about $4. My mother was amazed and indignant that anyone would pay for dust cloths. Of course, my mother can dust an entire house with one pair of old underwear. The Great Depression of the early 1930s was a harsh and brutal era that taught the parents of Radio Babies to save money and appreciate a steady paycheck, and the folks passed along the value of a buck to their children.

Because of that, job security has been a compelling need for many Radio Babies. Job-hopping is not a concept this age group understands or embraces. They were taught, "You get a job...you keep a job."

The Radio Babies I interviewed said these three factors most shaped their belief systems:

❏   Parents' views.

❏   Values held in their community.

❏   Views of respected political leaders.

Indeed, I've often heard my mother say, "The President said this on TV. It must be true." Imagine the shock and disbelief for many in this generation when Presidents Nixon and Clinton lied to them...on TV.

Baby Boomers

You know you're a Baby Boomer if...

❏   You thought you might one day join the Mickey Mouse Club.

❏   You knew who Elvis was before he wore sequins.

❏   Your favorite toy was a hula hoop, but you were never as good as your friends.

❏   You used a typewriter to write your term papers.

❏   You saw every episode of *Leave it to Beaver.*

❏   You are old enough to have watched man's first trip to the moon on TV and remember it.

❏   You remember Woodstock.

Some comments from the Baby Boomers we interviewed were:

I don't say "far out" anymore. But I still want to reach out far to fulfill my career dreams.

I have the house in the 'burbs and the white picket fence. I don't yet have everything I wanted to attain in the workplace.

I paid my dues along the way. Is it so much to ask for young people to make an occasional small sacrifice?!

I'm learning from the 60-plus crowd at work and I'm learning from the 20-somethings.

I've been through several bosses in my career, but it's hard when the boss is several years younger and short on experience!

Keep me interested or I'll leave and start my own company—I have the expertise to be your competitor.

Baby Boomers: A profile

My father came marching home from the Korean War in 1950. He and my mother celebrated his return in many ways, not the least of which was producing four Baby Boomer children in rapid succession. Consequently, I was used to a big family at home and large classes at school. There were a lot of us, so we learned early to compete for attention, rewards, and recognition.

Along with many of my generation, born between 1946 and 1964, I witnessed several revolutions in our country's culture during the 1960s and 1970s. Women gained access to "The Pill" as a means of birth control, and the sexual revolution was off and running. Every now and then I still feel a compulsion to burn an article of clothing. Dr. Martin Luther King, Jr. sparked a fire in African-Americans and Caucasians alike who wanted an end to racial discrimination. The civil rights movement blossomed in the 1960s and many Boomers marched side by side or waged sit-ins to protest segregation.

Like many of their Radio Baby parents, Boomers fought in a war outside U.S. borders. This time it was the Vietnam War, and it was markedly different from previous campaigns that called up young men and women. The Vietnam War was not popular in this country. The public could not support and rally behind President Johnson. Young men became conscientious objectors and fled the country. Survivors didn't often come home as heroes but instead were reviled at worst and dismissed at best. As a Boomer who lost a loved one in this war, I find it extremely painful to observe the disrespect and disdain to which many Vietnam vets are subjected.

Baby Boomers had heroes, just as did their parents. We looked up to people as diverse as Timothy Leary, John Glenn, and John F. and Bobby Kennedy. Boomer girls fell in love with John, Paul, George, or Ringo. We were sorely disappointed when, as teens or 20-somethings, a U.S. president (Nixon) lied to us on TV. We were more callous and older but wiser Americans by the time President Clinton looked into the TV camera and said, "I did not have sexual relations with that woman, Monica Lewinsky."

Baby Boomers are often characterized as ambitious, greedy, materialistic, aging flower children who channeled their energies into "making love, not war" before selling out in the 1980s. The Baby Boomers we interviewed were bemused by the stereotypes others hold of them, as people who marched against the Vietnam war in the '60s only to become the "suits" of the '80s. They told us there's much more to them than that.

Boomers are the most educated generation of the four discussed in this book (Knable 2001), and the objective of a higher education for many of the Boomers I interviewed was a better lifestyle. They said that their parents told them they could have anything they wanted. So they went for it—the American Dream.

There is a sizeable segment of the Baby Boomer generation, born between 1954 and 1965, that has begun lifting its voice as separate and apart from older Boomers. This group has begun referring to itself as Generation Jones, and admits to relating more to leisure suits, disco, aviator glasses, and KC and the Sunshine Band rather than the Beatles (McCaleb 2000).

The Boomers I interviewed said these influences shaped their perspectives most when they were growing up:

❏ Views of the immediate family (parents, aunts, uncles).

❏ Friends' values and views.

❏ Political events (such as Civil Rights marches).

Generation X

Robin:

You know you're a Gen Xer if...

❏ You wore shirts growing up that had an alligator or a guy on a horse on the chest, especially with your collar turned up.

❏ You remember the Atari and many hours of *Asteroids.*

❏ You couldn't wait until 1999 to play the song "1999" by Prince.

❏ One of your first favorite movies was *Star Wars* or *E.T.*

❏ Road trips with the family meant riding backwards in the station wagon.

❏ In high school and college, you lived for each new episode of *90210* and *Melrose Place.*

❏ You *totally* remember, like, the days of, like, "gag me with a spoon."

❏ You *do* know who shot J.R.

❏ "All skate" and "change directions" means something to you.

❏ You know what a rotary phone is.

❏ You actually owned and played records (*Grease* was a favorite).

❏ You typed your term papers on a word processor.

Some comments from the Gen Xers we interviewed were:

I have a family life...so sue me.

It's hard to manage people over 40 because they want to tell me what to do and how to do it. Not an option.

There's no reason I have to suffer in a suit and high heels all day just to look like someone's idea of a "professional." I work better if I'm comfy.

"We've always done it this way" is the Boomers' mantra.

Don't tell me one more time that you have under-wear older than me; that's gross!

I want respect for my years of college and techno-savvy—that should be worth something!

Hey, let's get creative in the workplace—I don't want my grandfather's incentive program!

State-of-the-art means today, not yesterday.

I'm tired of fixing the problems Boomers caused...and if I have to do that, let me do it my way!

Generation X: A profile

Though I don't personally remember it, we still have the home movies (not the VHS or DVD kind though) of me toddling around, with a TV in the background showing Neil Armstrong stepping on to the moon. So as far as I know, we've always had TVs and been able to go to the moon. But I did witness many dramatic changes in society, economy, and technology that shaped and created Generation X.

Those of us who are Gen Xers were born between 1965 and 1976 and represent the smallest segment of the population. We are the generation with the highest number of divorced parents, dual-income families, and rearing in a latchkey pro-gram. As a result, we learned very early to be independent and to fend for ourselves in order to survive.

Unlike the earlier generations, the individuals we looked up to could be found in the movies, on TV, or in a rock group. Even our president was a movie star. At some point, we all likely watched episodes of *The Brady Bunch*, *The Love Boat*, and *Happy Days*. And we knew who shot J.R., "where's the beef?" and of course, *Grease*.

Our economy has been recessed most of our lives as a result of oil shortages, terrorist attacks, and soaring inflation. We grew up scared and untrusting as a result of events such as Watergate, Iran Contra, the threat of nuclear warfare, bomb scares, Castro, and even AIDS.

We learned that politics never solved anything and usually made things worse. We quickly learned to not trust anyone or anything. The companies that our parents had worked for their entire lives were laying people off without an ounce of care for the employees. This taught us never to put all our eggs in one basket, but rather to keep our options open.

While the society and the economy were evolving and shaping our generation, technology was emerging in more areas than ever thought possible. In our lifetime, we've listened to music on records, eight-track tapes, cassettes, CDs, DVDs, MP3s, and more. We were the first generation entertained by video game systems such as Atari. We can't remember a time when we didn't have microwaves or TVs, but do know that the wattage and reception improved each year. Likewise, the prevalence of computers has taken off in our lifetime. It probably wasn't until our late teens or early 20s when they become a little more common than a typewriter or word processor, and today you can't live without one or two—or even three. In the meantime, we also watched the dawn and growth of the Internet, answering machines and voice mail, walkmans, boom boxes, beepers, cell phones, PDAs, and laptops. Basically, there is a machine that can help you to do anything you want anywhere you want.

The Generation Xers we interviewed said these three factors most shaped their belief systems:

❑ World events as seen on TV.

❑ Friends' values and views.

❑ A handful of respected coworkers.

Generation Y

You know you are a Gen Y if ...

❏ You typed your term paper on a computer, of course.

❏ You've always had an answering machine or voice mail.

❏ You grew up on video games—Nintendo, PlayStation, and even PC games.

❏ You were using a computer by the time you were learning to read.

❏ A record player is an antique and a CD is a given.

❏ You've always had cable TV with a remote control.

❏ You make your popcorn in the microwave, not on the stove.

❏ You've considered piercing something besides your ear.

❏ The Internet has existed as long as you remember.

Some comments from the Gen Ys we interviewed were:

So I have a pierced tongue...what does that have to do with my IQ?!

Doesn't anyone over 40 have values?

I can work just as effectively on a report at home; I don't have to drive through rush hour traffic to sit at my desk and get it done!

I want to go to work and feel safe. Is that too much to ask?

I'd like a mentor, not another mother or father.

Why should I pay someone's ideas of "dues" when I can deliver the goods?!

Generation Y: A profile

Generation Y, sometimes known as Generation Why, Millennials, and Echo Boomers, were born between 1977 and 1991. They are 60 million strong, which is three times the size of the Generation-Xers, and they were born in the fast lane!

As did the Generation Xers, Generation Y grew up with dual-income parents, divorces, and daycare. But this generation grew up under very different parenting styles. Timeouts became a popular method for discipline and spankings became viewed as child abuse. Parents began protecting their children from the woes the world was throwing at them.

As a result, this generation has a very different perspective on many things:

❑ They are extremely conscious of the environment. They worry about our future, not just locally, but globally, and actively engage in and encourage acts of recycling and reducing wastes or pollutants.

❑ They are a diverse generation with an open mind and acceptance for differences in race, gender, ethnicity, sexual orientation, and so on.

❑ They are also an extremely expressive generation as evidenced by some of their dress, body jewelry, and brightly colored hair.

❑ They are very socially conscious and committed to any cause they value. Volunteering for their cause is important to them.

❑ Morally, interviews showed them to be much more against premarital and unprotected sex, alcohol, and drugs than Baby Boomers or Gen Xers.

Gen Ys continue to report that their number one concern is personal safety. This generation did not grow up in the times when kids freely played outside without supervision. They were taught to fear strangers outside and even inside the home (in other words, kidnappings from your bed), never to go anywhere alone, and never to trust anyone.

They've seen assassinations, school shootings, and wars televised live with every detail disclosed on TV. They watched terrorists attack their country and many others. They saw a president lie on TV and continue his political role with only a smack on his hand from the media. And they continue to live in fear of AIDS, anthrax, and other biogenetic warfare.

At the same time, they've lived through one of the biggest booms in the economic history of the United States, a time when even a teenager could get a part-time job in a technology role making more money than his or her parents. Many of them even started their own businesses at a very young age and aspire to be entrepreneurs the rest of their lives.

But an even bigger impact on this generation is technology! According to Teenage Research Unlimited, more than 80 percent of teenagers have Internet access, whether at home, school, work, a friend's home, or the library. A recent study by the Fortino Group further predicts that current 10- to 17-year-olds will spend a third of their lives (about 23 years) on the Internet.

As far as this generation knows, every household has a computer, CD player, VCR, and video games. Not only do their parents have beepers and cell phones, but so did they as teenagers. They've grown up on the new wave of video games that are virtually based, where they've adapted strengths in strategizing and troubleshooting problems instantly…or you're out of the game. Many of their video games are "online," where they can compete against other players all over the world. All this technology enables them to be much more globally minded than our past generations. Thanks to the Internet and instant messaging, many have instant pen pals all over the world that they can chat with at any hour of the day or night.

The Generation Ys we interviewed said these three factors most shaped their belief systems:

❑ Community values and lifestyles.

❑ Grandparents' views.

❑ World events as seen on TV.

Summary

Linda and Robin:

As we were growing up, many factors influenced our approach to the world of work: parents, teachers, friends, family, and events occurring around us. Radio Babies who grew up during the Great Depression and WWII were profoundly affected by rationing and doing without basic necessities. Baby Boomers, on the other hand, grew up during a time of prosperity in the United States and came to believe they could "have it all." Gen Xers came of age when technology was helping people live easier lives, but the world and all its troubles was in their living room via TV, Internet, and telephone. Gen Y has emerged into a world where school shootings, terrorism, and an environment at risk are part and parcel of daily life. Small wonder, then, that Gen Y is desirous of a workplace that can assure employees' safety and wellbeing. Astute employers understand these differences across the generations and will tailor their employee relations activities to meet these different needs.

Case Study: Career Goals

The head of a school administration department has an outstanding administrative assistant. He sees a great deal of potential in the assistant to grow and become even more than an administrative assistant. She is young and has three school-aged children. She has taken this job to be able to work and be with her children after school and during the summer. She just wants to put in her time. Her boss, on the other hand, is focused on the company (the school) first and doesn't realize that employees can balance work and family life if employers are willing to be flexible. The differing work perspectives are frustrating to both individuals.

Question for Discussion

1. How would you coach the two of them to make this win-win for them both?

Solution

In this scenario, the head of the school has a career plan for the employee but hasn't considered the employee's career goals in making that plan. Obviously, this is a high-potential and successful employee, or the head of the school wouldn't have such high aspirations for her.

Rather than making judgments and decisions on what she should do, the manager should be providing this positive feedback to the employee and including her in development and career planning. It will require him to be open-minded and listen to what she likes and dislikes about the job and what her developmental plans would be.

The career goals the head of the school may have for this employee may not be the same as the employee's own goals. But the discussion will provide feedback to the employee on the great job she is doing, and allow the head of the school and employee to develop a mutually beneficial plan. There may actually be a way for the school to benefit from the strengths of the employee while not requiring her to sacrifice what she wants out of her job/school hours.

Unfortunately, in this situation, the head of the school continued to stay focused on trying to push the employee to follow his career goals for her. As a result, she chose to quit, indicating that family time was more important to her than a career.

Chapter 4

How to Entice Each Generation to Join Your Organization

Linda:

My first "real job" after college took me to Japan to work for the U.S. Civil Service. The magnet that drew me to that job was the opportunity to travel and live outside the country. I came back to the United States with excellent experience and several options for my next job. I took my time, though, as many of my friends who were my age did, to find an organization where the opportunities for a status job and "perks" were high. After all, I had big plans for a (large) house in the 'burbs with a Mercedes parked in one side of the two-car garage! That was then. Now, I wouldn't even consider joining an organization for money or status alone, although both are still important aspects of work.

Robin:

When I graduated from college, I was fortunate to have two job offers. One position was on a human resources development program for which I rotated through the different aspects of human resources in different locations and businesses in order to get as much experience as I could. The other position, paying $15,000–$20,000 more, would be as a HR generalist in a small plant. This was a no-brainer for me—it isn't about money...it's about quick, hands-on experience with instant feedback and an opportunity to grow very rapidly in the organization. Plus, the experience would be extremely transferable for my next position/company. I took the lower-paying position with the better opportunity for hands-on experience.

The research results—Radio Babies

Linda:

In its study titled "Valuing Older Workers," the American Association of Retired Persons describes older workers as having better judgment, a stronger commitment to quality, lower turnover, and more reliable attendance than younger workers. If this is the case, it's smart business for employers to have a balance between younger and older employees. It's also smart business to tailor recruiting methods and messages to each generation.

Almost half of the Radio Babies I interviewed expressed a desire for flexible benefits that can be tailored to their needs. (Much has been said about Gen Xers demanding this feature from potential employers, but older workers want flexibility too!) Many of these people even said they'd actually move to another company if that would enable them to receive the specific benefits they need. This is coming from a generation that couldn't be moved by dynamite in years past!

I asked interviewees what benefits are important at this stage in their lives, and there's certainly consistency across their answers. In highest demand are:

- ❏ Long-term care insurance.
- ❏ Coverage for short-term stays in nursing homes (for themselves or their spouse).
- ❏ Employee assistance programs that provide grief counseling.

Several people commented that companies that offer only benefits such as tuition reimbursement, daycare, or maternity/paternity leave are missing an opportunity to entice seasoned, experienced workers to join their organization. They encouraged employers to consider different benefit tiers or "cafeteria" benefits.

Not surprisingly, almost 40 percent of the interviewed Radio Babies said they'd join a company that provided at least some promise of job security. Many of these people said they'd stay in the workforce until age 70 or longer, *if* the company would agree to a reduction in hours or short layoffs before automatically firing senior employees when times get tough. Salary isn't typically a big issue for these folks. Being productive and staying active are their primary concerns.

The third reason Radio Babies in the study said they'd "jump ship" was to work for a company that appreciates and calls upon their experience. This group was quick to point out that they fully expect to keep their skills current. They don't expect to apply 1970 experiences to the realities of today. One person said, "Just once, I'd love it if a 30-year-old would say, 'What do you think— what has your experience taught you?'" Many interviewees told me they'd jump at the chance to work for an organization that includes and involves them on task forces, focus groups, and problem-solving teams. That doesn't seem to be too much to ask. As a wise person once said, "A mind is a terrible thing to waste."

The research results—Baby Boomers

According to U.S. Census statistics, people older than 50 will make up 42 percent of the population by 2010. The Boomers are getting older, and organizations should begin planning *now* to find and keep quality Boomers, instead of losing them to retirement (or the competition).

Almost 40 percent of the interviewed Boomers said three features, in this order, would entice them to join a company: salary, title, and status. Many Boomers told me they're *still* paying for their piece of the American Dream. That's because many of them took a very big piece. So a good salary is still of paramount importance to many of them.

Some of the interviewees are locked into paying for children in college and parents in nursing homes. No wonder Boomers are often called "the sandwich generation"! Even if the children are out of school, the trend now is for these "boomerangers" to move back home. They can't afford to live as well as their parents did right out of college, so they live at home until they can save enough to live the lifestyle to which they became accustomed growing up.

About a fourth of the Boomers interviewed said benefits are a key factor in their decision to join a company. They're interested in different benefits than when they were 25 of course, but benefits are a significant factor nonetheless. Interestingly, benefits that provide a good work–life balance, such as the opportunity to telecommute, are important to Boomers (you thought only the younger folks wanted this, right?!). Everyone has a need to pull out of the "rat race" occasionally.

The research results—Generation X

Robin:

Who will work tomorrow when the Radio Babies and Baby Boomers ultimately do retire? Though we want to do all we can to retain these two generations in the workplace, we also need to consider the needs and values of the remaining generations.

Not surprisingly, when we surveyed individuals from Generation X, we found family happiness and a balance between work and life to be at the top of their list of what is important. Given their history of being latchkey children or raised in broken homes, it isn't surprising that family happiness and work–life balance are at the top. Also at the top was feeling safe. And as we discussed earlier, Gen Xers have also seen their family, friends, and country experience a great deal of threat from terrorists and disease over their years, not to mention politics. The Gen Xers we spoke to continually express mistrust of people in political office, and are concerned that unqualified, unethical people were and are in important positions.

To ensure we make the right connection between what is important to Gen Xers and what entices them to join an organization, we asked! We observed that finding a match between company and personal values is the number one issue. So they are interviewing you as much as you are interviewing them to see if they even *want* to work for you. The next most common answer was a salary and benefits package. Note, it is salary *and* benefits package. For Gen Xers, it is the entire package—not just the money. They want to know how much they will be paid combined with what time off they will have and what healthcare programs you have. For Gen Xers, it is about the total compensation package relative to what's important to them. Finally, the third response we received was growth and development opportunities. Gen Xers are not chasing titles and status but expansion of their knowledge, skills, and abilities. Their loyalty is to their profession and how diverse they can make their skillset.

So as you begin evaluating your culture to determine if it is a fit for Gen Xers, ask yourself these questions:

- ❏ Do you provide feedback and credit for individual results?
- ❏ Do you have a meaningful mission that is shared with all employees, and do you en sure they have a clear understanding of how they can contribute to the accomplishment of the mission?
- ❏ Do you provide your employees with an opportunity to share their ideas or provide input?
- ❏ Do your supervisors roll up their sleeves and act as leaders—not managers?
- ❏ Do you have a fun work environment that makes everyone excited to be at work?

❏ Do you offer multiple strategies and paths to help your employees develop their careers?

❏ Does your company truly support activities t that ensure a good work–life balance?

Based on our research, if you can answer yes to the majority of these questions, you are on the right path to attracting and retaining Gen Xers. If you can't answer yes to most of these questions, you may need to make some changes to your culture in order to be more in line with the needs of Gen Xers. In addition, you will find these are many of the same things employees of other generations will begin requesting as well, but for their own reasons.

The research results—Generation Y

Generation Y was described as "the most demanding generation in history," by Bruce Tulgan and Dr. Carolyn Martin in *Managing the Generation Mix—Part II.* I've also heard Gen Ys called "Generation X on steroids." Gen Ys are very similar to Gen Xers, but they are also very different, based on the research we did.

When we asked 500 Gen Ys what was most important to them, the top three responses were quality friendships, feeling they can make a contribution on the job, and a feeling of safety. They like an organization in which they can create friendships much as they did growing up in school. The organizations that have a social flair are what will catch their eye. Some examples include company leagues (such as golf or basketball) or company social events (such as opening night of *The Matrix* or meeting after work for coffee or a beer). But these quality relationships must go hand in hand with feeling that what they do adds value to the organization.

Recognizing what is important to a Gen Y isn't enough if you don't incorporate some of the key things that entice them to join an organization. During our research, we found the top three ways to get a Gen Y to join an organization were salary, a friendly and casual work environment, and growth and development opportunities—in that order. It isn't surprising that salary was on top given the money that was thrown around in the late '90s when the first Gen Ys were entering the workforce. With the enormous labor shortage predicted for the next five to 10 years, high salaries and signing bonuses are likely to continue. But it isn't all about money. Gen Ys need to enjoy where they are working—in a fun atmosphere, minus the stuffy blue suits. And as the Gen Xers do, they want to see opportunities to improve their skills, knowledge, and abilities through on-the-job experiences, mentorships, training, and otherwise learning from others.

The Gen Ys constitute a large pool of talent eager to be groomed for the workforce and ready to fill in the gaps we are sure to encounter. They will eagerly jump ship to go to work for a company that offers them the opportunity share their valuable ideas and input with respect, because this will allow them to grow and to feel that they contribute to the bottom line. And the company must demonstrate that it will provide them with an opportunity to develop their career. Organizations will need to not only provide the framework for career growth, but will also have to find ways to advertise the success of those programs in order to continue to attract others. A company may find this easier if it can demonstrate its integrity and values by offering a quality service or product.

Again, you need to evaluate your culture to see if it is a fit for Gen Ys. Ask yourself these questions:

❏ Do you provide positive and constructive feedback more often than annually?

❏ Do you help all employees understand how they contribute to the organization's success?

❏ Do you have a friendly, fun work environment where work is play?

❏ Does your organization make every effort to invest in the development of its employees and make it well-known to everyone?

❏ Does the organization have a strong level of integrity and commitment to quality service and products?

Again, if you can answer yes to the majority of these questions, you are on the right path to attracting and retaining Gen-Ys. If not, you may need to make some changes to your culture in order to be more in line with the needs of Gen Ys. Other organizations are doing it, and you will lose talent if you don't.

Recruiting methods across the generations

Linda:

First, let's talk about recruiting methods for members of the Radio Baby and Boomer generations. When we talk about recruiting methods for Generations X and Y, we'll emphasize and encourage the use of technology. For the two older generations, however, a balance between high-tech and traditional recruiting methods will be necessary to attract workers.

Radio Babies and Boomers still read the classified section of the newspaper and trade or professional journals. Baby Boomers tend to network and do the "meet and greet thing" at professional association meetings. The Radio Babies I interviewed are very comfortable with a structured outplacement approach or working through an executive search agency to help them sell their years of service without appearing "too old" for the job. Boomers and Radio Babies alike told me, "Tell people to send job notices to churches. We still attend regularly."

It's important to tailor your advertising medium to different age groups. It's just as important to tailor your recruiting message. The Boomers and Radio Babies in our research encouraged companies that want to hire them to deliver this message loud and clear:

- ❏ We appreciate and value your experience.
- ❏ We want to use your expertise.
- ❏ We need you.

In addition, they want to know the specifics about the job—exactly what they will do and what are the perks that will go with it.

Here is a sample ad that would be an excellent draw for both Boomers and Radio Babies:

COMPANY, a successful and growth-oriented leader in the fast-paced, quickly expanding modular assembly segment of the American automotive industry, has an immediate opening for a seasoned Plant Controller at our new, $200-plus million engine dress and sequencing facility.

Job Overview

This successful individual (along with the Plant Manager and the Plant Engineering Manager) will become a member of the operation's three-person executive management team, which has full P&L responsibility for the $200-plus million assembly distribution facility. As such, the Plant Controller will play an active role in developing, monitoring, and achieving the operation's annual goals through its ongoing continuous improvement activities, while providing financial, analytical, and decision-making leadership to the 200-plus local team members. This is a career-level position with unending responsibility that will provide great personal satisfaction for a mature individual that likes to work, functions well in a team environment, and enjoys spending time "on the production floor" observing, analyzing, questioning, discussing, teaching, and leading others in order to continually improve operational performance.

Desired Qualifications and Experience

We are seeking a seasoned manager who has gained considerable working knowledge in a manufacturing or distribution facility that provides the applicant:

- ❑ Expertise in the design and implementation of internal control systems, such as QS-9000;

- ❑ Proficiency in effectively managing high-dollar inventories in a fast-paced, just-in-time environment;

- ❑ The interpersonal skills, personal comfort, and respect for other people that are necessary to effectively communicate and actively interface with a production workforce on a daily basis;

- ❑ The desire to strive for both personal and operational excellence through a neverending search for a better tomorrow.

Minimum Requirements

- ❑ Bachelor's degree in Business, Accounting, or Finance

- ❑ 15 years' post-degree experience in the business world

- ❑ 10 years' experience in manufacturing or an inventory-related field

❏ 5 years' experience and demonstrated success as a Plant Controller in a manufacturing or distribution facility

❏ Significant involvement in Materials Management or Inventory Control

❏ Proficient using Microsoft Office, with expertise in Excel

❏ ERP experience (preferably using QAD)

❏ Working knowledge of Information Technologies systems in the workplace

❏ Work experience for a privately owned company is a plus

❏ Creative, self-motivated, and works well in a cross-functional team environment

❏ Excellent interpersonal communication skills and well organized

❏ Committed to achieving world-class performance standards

Responsibilities of the Plant Controller

❏ Integral Leadership Role on Plant Management Team

❏ Lead, manage, develop, and hold organization accountable

❏ Monitor and manage all aspects of the plant's inventory to ensure correct quantities are available when required

❏ Monitor weekly cycle counts for material variances and proper levels

❏ Monitor engineering change process and controls

❏ Lead physical inventories and resolve any variances

- ❏ Prepare annual operating budget and monthly forecast based upon actual performance and changing customer needs
- ❏ Overall financial responsibility for the operation and all related activities
- ❏ Monthly financial reporting and financial analysis to the owners
- ❏ Update and track plant "key measures"
- ❏ All accounting functions
- ❏ Payrolls, time/attendance and benefits administration
- ❏ Control system design and implementation; report writing
- ❏ Internal auditing to COMPANY's business system and internal controls
- ❏ Provide the corporate sales team assistance in new business efforts by providing quotation and estimating expertise
- ❏ Act as the in-house information technology ("IT") manager as a liaison to the corporate IT team
- ❏ Effectively manage all business risks.

COMPANY offers a full range of competitive benefits and prides itself in being a great place to work.

If you are interested in this career position and feel that your skills and abilities are consistent with those outlined above, please mail your resume and salary requirements to...

Yes, it's a lot of information. But folks in the older generations are looking for the specifics, and for an organization that wants and will respect someone who is seasoned. Although you may not need this much detail, it gives you an idea of what you need to think about including.

Robin:

The key to a competitive and successful workforce is diversity: a workforce that includes individuals from all the generations. This means you need a variety of recruiting methods to attract folks across all the generations.

Though many of the traditional methods we mentioned will hit everyone, especially the Radio Babies and Baby Boomers, it will take sharp technology and advertising to ensure you are attracting individuals from Generations X and Y.

For the most part, these two younger generations are going to take advantage of every ounce of technology to make their job search easier, and a success. You'll need to advertise the job on multiple online job posting boards—local, national, trade-related, or all three. Plus, you will definitely want to create a job posting board on your company's Website. The job posting board will need to provide an easy and responsive way for candidates to apply online, and be regularly updated.

Where you advertise isn't the only thing you'll need to do differently. Gone are the days of receiving resumes via snail mail. With the advancements of technology, these techno-savvy generations like to apply immediately and get a response immediately. You will need to have a human resources e-mail address and/or an online application process. For the process to succeed, you must have someone regularly checking the applications/resumes and following up with candidates. Otherwise, your credibility will be shot from the get-go.

The actual copy of the ads will be critical as well. Gen Xers and Gen Ys like short, snappy copy that gets right to the point of what they will be doing. You'll need to include the key words that will attract these individuals to your ads when they do online searches. The ad will need to be dedicated to advertising the culture of your organization as it relates to the values of these two generations. As described in *Dynamics of the Multigenerational Workplace*, "If you are ready to create a fun, flexible, educational, non-micromanaged work atmosphere where Xers have a variety of projects to engage them, you'll have Generation X beating down the door to go to work for you." To do this, your ads will need to include key words such as:

- ❏ Fast-paced.
- ❏ Individual contribution.
- ❏ Work–life balance.
- ❏ Family-friendly.
- ❏ Do it your way.
- ❏ Opportunity to grow.
- ❏ No rules.
- ❏ State-of-the-art technology.

Only list these kinds of features in your ad if you truly offer them. Otherwise, you'll get to experience how fast these generations will leave an organization that doesn't fulfill its promises.

Here are a few sample ads we think would be excellent draws for Gen Xers and Ys.

Got game? So do we. We're a 75-year-old design/branding agency with the metabolism of a 4-year-old. Come play where design is a competitive weapon. Come play in the house of COMPANY. If descriptions of your game include "gifted," "amazing," and "inspired"—this is your lucky day. All you need is 5–7 years of client service experience in a design/advertising agency, the presentation skills to sell ice to Eskimos in winter, and a love of the game of branding. You'll have strategic perspective, an appreciation of what great design can do for a brand, and the ability to lead your clients there. We look forward to hearing from you. Send your resume and cover letter, including salary requirements, to: hr@COMPANY.com.

LET'S FACE IT—YOU DON'T LIVE TO WORK; YOU WORK TO LIVE! COMPANY recognizes the importance of a work–life–family balance and we take pride in fostering an atmosphere that recognizes and promotes personal growth and development! If there's one thing we're NOT, it's a typical mortgage company! If teamwork, support, positive energy, and personal growth are things you value, you just might be a fit for our team!

$100,000. That dollar figure represents a VERY REALISTIC annual earnings potential when you become a Loan Consultant at COMPANY. Candidates must be hard-working, driven, professional, and exhibit superior communication skills!

TEAMWORK. At COMPANY, it's not just a concept; it's a way of life. Whoever said "the whole is greater than the sum of its parts" knew what he was talking about.

PERKS, ANYONE? Our employees deserve the best. That's why we offer a top-notch, comprehensive benefits program as well as a fabulous compensation structure. Medical, dental, life and disability insurance, as well as a 401K/profit sharing plan are just a few of the perks that come along with being part of the COMPANY team. And we haven't even mentioned the work–life balance programs and fun contests and giveaways that have become core elements of our corporate culture. Need we say more?

REQUIREMENTS: 2–3 years proven sales experience in your respective field is preferred, but motivated, hardworking candidates with no sales experience will be considered as well. Mortgage lending/broker experience NOT required! Must embrace our shared corporate values such as open-mindedness, good character, positive attitude, and motivation to succeed! COMPANY values and maintains a culture committed to teamwork, mutual support, dedication, and fun. We always work hard, and always celebrate successes!

COMPANY provides a comprehensive, top-notch training program that is second to none in the industry! We will also arrange and equip employees for their state loan officer licensing requirements. We provide an aggressive commission structure, outstanding benefits, leads, and the latest industry technology to make your six-figure dreams a reality! If you're SERIOUS about getting compensated for your RESULTS, then E-MAIL your resume, with cover letter, to: jobs@COMPANY.org. Visit our Website! *www.COMPANY.com*. Why would you work anywhere else?

Summary

The "hook" that draws people into your organization will be shaped differently for each generation. Older Baby Boomers are now less attracted to status and money; however, these incentives can still be highly effective. Radio Babies can be enticed to come back into the workplace if they can enjoy flexible hours and benefits. Gen Xers often gravitate towards companies with a mission and vision that connects with their own life goals and desires. Gen Ys, still finding their place in the world of work, are more likely to start their own company so they can make their stamp on U.S. industry. Placing the typical one-paragraph ad in the classified section of the local newspaper may be a waste of time and money. The message—and the way it's communicated—must be tailored for maximum results.

Figure 4-1: Recruitment strategies by generation

Radio Babies and Boomers	Gen Xers and Gen Ys
Stress "value experiences" and "use your expertise"	Short, snappy copy
Detailed description of job	Stress fast-paced, individual contributions, work–life balance, opportunity to grow
Traditional methods: classified ads, churches, meet-and-greets, outplacement firms, recruiting agencies	Technological methods: job boards, company Websites, association job boards

Case Study: Recruiting

The hiring manager for a dynamic, creative organization needs to hire for an administrative position with a strong emphasis on data entry and computer skills. The hiring manager wants the position to be advertised in the Sunday newspaper. She does not want the ad to disclose the company name or provide the company address, just a P.O. box, and definitely no e-mail address.

The hiring manager isn't against hiring anyone of any particular age group but assumes the right candidate will likely be younger with strong computer skills.

Question for Discussion

1. How would you advise her on sourcing candidates for this administrative position?

Solution

Bridging the generation gap requires us to realize that what works for our generation isn't what works for all generations. This 60-year-old hiring manager grew up with newspaper advertising and blind company ads. Those days are gone for all generations, but especially if you are trying to fill a position requiring any technological skill.

To fill this position, you need to think like the individual that will be doing the administrative work and data entry. Will he or she be looking in the newspaper classifieds or online? Will he or she take the time to respond via snail mail? Better yet, will he or she want to work for a company that doesn't use technology for advertising job openings?

Searching for candidates doesn't have to be expensive, but it does require some thought. For this position, we'd definitely advise against the newspaper ad unless the hiring manager got a great deal that combined the classified ad with an online ad. To find someone with computer skills, you need to use online job boards. This may require searching a resume bank or posting a job in a national or local service. Also, consider some nontraditional options such as local schools or associations. Your cost per hire will be much lower!

Chapter 5

Retaining Quality Radio Babies

Linda:

My husband didn't want to retire, not really. But there was nothing new and exciting to try. No one seemed to need his advice. Getting dressed to go to work each day became too daunting a task. So he retired at 55, and now the man is driving his family nuts because he has too much time on his hands!

This situation appears to be widespread, judging from our interviews and current discussions with Baby Boomer clients. Workers in their 50s and 60s may not truly want to retire; however, they're not energized to come to work every day unless they receive new challenges and opportunities. We'd like to offer some suggestions to avoid losing this talented segment of the workforce before they're really ready to retire.

Anyone who believes that Radio Babies do not have the energy and will to contribute to the workplace should visit my home: You'll find a restless man with a working brain and lots of ideas to share! My interviews with other Radio Babies tracked with what I see at home—I didn't meet anyone who fit the unfortunate stereotype of slow-moving, withdrawn, uninterested people.

What will it take to retain an older workforce that has wisdom, energy, and loyalty to spare? In this chapter, I'll share the insights I gained from talking with Radio Babies all over the country.

Myth #1: Older workers are afraid of change

Radio Babies also want employers to know that loyalty to a company—or to an idea—doesn't mean they're afraid of change or just sitting comfortably on their laurels. If working for an organization has been a positive experience that has afforded growth opportunities and challenges for employees, then that company deserves acknowledgement and loyalty in return. Even in bad times for the company. The people I interviewed want the rest of us to know that they're willing to adapt ideas and work methods *for a sound reason*. If change is indeed necessary, they said, they're willing to learn new techniques and approaches...really.

The oldest Radio Babies are in their 70s, and many are retired. But some of them are actively working more hours and more productively than any other employee in their respective companies. At the same time, the youngest of this generation have just turned 60 and still have several potential years of productivity and workplace contributions left in them, especially if they too don't plan to retire from working just yet.

Fully 60 percent of the 500 older workers I interviewed want to stay in the workplace until they're at least 65. And 25 percent would put off their imminent retirement *if* their companies treated them differently. Any employer would be crazy to not hire a dedicated, loyal employee whom you know you'd have for at least two to five years, given the average tenure of employees nowadays.

Almost a third of the participants in my study said they want to see tangible signs that their experience and expertise are valued. The signs they're searching for are:

❏ Inclusion in strategic planning, directly or indirectly.

❏ Involvement in focus groups or task forces on technical topics.

❏ Involvement in focus groups or task forces on establishing a diversity initiative that includes different age groups.

❏ The opportunity to mentor other (not necessarily younger) employees.

❏ Requests to write articles on behalf of the company for journals and periodicals.

❏ Opportunity to speak on the company's behalf at conferences and conventions.

Myth #2: Radio Babies are too old to work

More than any other impression they want to dispel, Radio Babies want younger people to know that they may be physically slower, but their brains are still moving at warp speed. Medical technology has allowed for 60-year-olds to feel healthy longer and act much younger than people of the same age 100 years ago. I'm sure you've heard the phrase "40 is the new 20." I like that sentiment. Radio Babies have seen enormous and exciting changes in the world around them from the time they were children, and they've adapted and worked through all these changes. Why wouldn't Radio Babies continue to adapt to change?

Notice that these activities represent more than nodding in older workers' direction occasionally. They comprise meaningful ways that people can contribute to the organization's objectives.

Perhaps you're a manager who is younger than 40 and supervise a workforce that's in their 50s or even 60s. Do you sometimes feel members of another generation are from a different planet? Not to worry, we all have those "generational moments." We'll cover this in detail in Chapter 11, but for now, here are some suggestions for effective interaction with direct reports (employees reporting directly to you) who are older than you:

- ❏ Acknowledge their experience.
- ❏ Listen to their ideas. They still read. They still observe. They know things.
- ❏ Provide hands-on experience for learning new technology. They'll get it.
- ❏ Provide recognition for their contributions. A personal visit to their work station is good. A written note or letter is great!

Almost 30 percent of those I interviewed said that flexibility in benefits that would meet their unique needs would entice them to stay with an organization. For Radio Babies, a benefit program that provides an opportunity to periodically enroll in different options is key. In 1998, employees in this generation may have needed health insurance for their children in graduate school. Now, a pressing need may be for an excellent vision care program. Five years in the future, this group may need long-term care insurance for themselves and their spouses.

The older workers I talked with also want the benefit of ongoing education and training. The opportunity to be constantly challenged and mentally stimulated is a significant retention tool. There is no empirical evidence that adults lose their ability to learn past age 50 (or 60 for that matter). Think of major contributors to our society who were older than 50 at the time of some of their important accomplishments: Ben Franklin, George Burns, Picasso, and Bob Hope. None of these people retired early!

Another benefit desired by Radio Babies is the option of telecommuting. Not all jobs and personalities are suited for work at home, of course, but for those positions that are amenable, why not try out telecommuting on a pilot basis? Be sure to set clear expectations about results and use of company-owned equipment. Build in some "face time" at the office so telecommuters still feel connected to the company. Telecommuting options help the company manage space and work efficiently while helping older workers transition into retirement.

The Radio Babies I interviewed assured me they would put in extra hours at no pay or try new work processes and technology to allow their company to survive and thrive. In other words, this is a segment of the workforce that wants to be part of the solution.

They'll stick with a company during hard times. What a resource: like money in the bank!

According to the Census Bureau, 21 million U.S. citizens turned 55 or older by 2005, and the projected population age 45 and older by 2010 is just more than 121 million! At least 81 million of these people will be between 45 and 64, and very likely to be interested in working in some capacity. Good thing, because there are only 34 million Gen Xers coming along after the Boomers to fill all their jobs! Ironically, the Equal Employment Opportunity Commission (EEOC) reports that the number of age discrimination complaints filed in 2002 was 25 percent higher than in 2000.

It's smart business to proactively build retention plans that target mature employees into our human resource management practices. And it's the right thing to do for our country to remain loyal to the population segment that Tom Brokaw has dubbed "the greatest generation" (Brokaw 2001).

How do we retain quality workers in the Radio Baby generation? We start by looking at people's abilities and potential, instead of looking at a number.

Summary

Quality employees with years of wisdom don't all have to leave the workplace! Some members of the Radio Baby generation remain energetic and enthusiastic about their careers. Many are still fully capable—and willing—of learning new approaches and to operate in a world of technology. The keys to retaining older workers are respect and inclusion. Respect their experience and include them in planning for your organization's future. This generation wants to leave a meaningful legacy. It's to your advantage to let them.

Case Study: Hiring Older Workers

You are an HR director working for a highly successful manufacturing firm in the Midwest. The firm is searching for a new administrative assistant to serve as the receptionist and perform other general administrative duties. You've identified a highly skilled professional individual in her late 50s who was recommended by a customer of the company. She meets all the requirements of the job the CEO has specified, except one: "young and spunky." Along with the challenge of explaining the legal implications of this final requirement, you want to persuade the CEO to consider this talented candidate.

Question for Discussion

1. What can you do to demonstrate to the CEO that he should openly consider this candidate regardless of her age?

Solution

As the HR director it is your responsibility to ensure the company operates in compliance with the local, state, and federal laws. To ensure compliance by all managers, including the CEO, the HR director will need to overview the Age Discrimination Employment Act and the subsequent potential cost if a discrimination case is brought against the company—and, even further, won.

As important as compliance with the law is, the HR director also needs to get to the bottom of what the CEO is really looking for when he says "young and spunky," which is not a true job requirement. By focusing on the job requirements, the HR director can compare the candidate to these requirements. If she has the qualifications, the HR director should encourage the CEO to at least meet with the candidate for a face-to-face interview to assess her skills relative to the job requirements identified. In addition, the CEO and/or HR director could conduct a reference check with the customer who referred her to them, asking pointed job-related questions.

In this particular scenario, the HR consultant followed these suggestions. As a result, the candidate was hired for the position and the CEO still raves about how happy he is with hiring her. She's perfect for the job, the customers love her, and she is very committed and loyal to the position and company.

Chapter 6

Retaining Quality Baby Boomers

Linda:

"By 2012, the group of workers aged 55 and older will grow to 19.1 percent of the total workforce," says Leslie Stevens-Huffman in her article "Could Your Best New Hire be a 'Recareering Boomer'?" (Stevens-Huffman 2005). And according to James

L'Allier, Ph.D., and Kenneth Kolosh in "Preparing for Baby Boomer Retirement," 79 percent of Boomers plan to work in some capacity during their retirement years (L'Allier 2005). Do you want the best and the brightest in this age group working for *your* company? Now is the time to establish a work environment that compels them to stay.

I'm often asked if it's really possible to satisfy driven, relentlessly materialistic, "I want it all" Baby Boomers.

Sure.

In this chapter, I'll share what so many of us Boomers call "the bottom line": what it takes to keep us as contributing members of your organization.

Myth #3: Baby Boomers can't handle technology

Baby Boomers often face challenge from younger generations who think they're not willing or capable of learning technology. As a matter of fact, the youngest Boomers (born in the early '60s) remind us that they grew up with technology just as much as the Gen Xers. The older Boomers remind us that if they can organize and lead a civil rights movement, if they can protect the country in times of war, and if they can build on the infrastructure their parents started, they can certainly learn how to operate a PDA.

Almost 40 percent of my interviewees spoke fervently about their desire for continuing opportunities for career advancement. This doesn't necessarily equate with promotions and executive management positions. For many, career advancement means job enhancement, job rotation, or short-term assignments and projects. Many of the Boomers I talked with readily acknowledge that their companies have a finite number of positions at the top. That doesn't mean that one's career development must stagnate. That doesn't mean that pursuit of the American Dream must come to a dead stop at age 40.

Just to ignite some brainstorming in your company, here are some ideas for potential short- or long-term assignments that can provide a challenge and stimulate enthusiasm:

❏ Benchmark and analyze strategic planning methods of three to five global organizations. Present the results to colleagues.

❏ Facilitate the strategic planning sessions of a division within the organization other than your own.

❏ Join a task force whose mission is to develop a performance management process that supports execution of the company's strategic plan.

❏ Champion a continuous improvement recommendation or a process-improvement team.

❏ Develop a communications plan to advise employees of a change in product, procedures, or processes.

❏ Facilitate employee meetings to solicit process-improvement ideas.

❏ Develop and deliver a training session on the company's core values.

❏ Facilitate roundtables with the company's business units to help them identify their competitive differentiators.

❏ Develop a contingency plan to be put in place if a key supplier goes out of business.

❏ Serve on a new project or product review committee.

❏ Assess the last group of incoming customer surveys to generate ideas for new approaches or products.

❏ Interview vendors about their trends and issues; develop a collaborative approach towards addressing those trends for competitive advantage.

❏ Learn a second language; teach to one or more colleagues.

❏ Collaborate with human resources to create a rewards and recognition system that reinforces interdependent, joint goals.

❏ Facilitate an internal/external team with suppliers to shorten cycle times, reduce bottlenecks, or improve responsiveness to customers.

A fifth of the Boomers in our study want respect for their experience and expertise. Does this sound familiar? It was the top answer among Radio Babies as well.

The Boomers want respect demonstrated in tangible ways such as inclusion on task forces and involvement in mentor programs. A common thread among Boomers surfaced: They expect to earn respect by demonstrating their capabilities. They wish younger coworkers would at least give them a chance to show why "this can work—try it."

Myth #4: Baby Boomers are too bossy

Boomers want younger workers to understand that they truly don't believe they can treat you as they do their children (and therefore tell you what to do)! Boomers do, however, want to share their experiences and lessons learned to save younger people from making the same painful mistakes. Boomers didn't like their own (perceived) older coworkers' bossiness either, and certainly rebelled socially and politically in their youth. Their "word to the wise" is advice—not an order.

The biggest complaint I heard from Boomers is that workers in their 20s and early 30s automatically dismiss them instead of operating on the belief that experience may have been a good teacher. Boomers were taught to work hard and "pay their dues." Now they feel that some "dues" are owed them for this long-term effort.

Although salary, status, and title may compel Baby Boomers to join an organization, what keeps them is much different. Just fewer than 20 percent of Boomers said they want to stay with their companies—as long as the work continues to be interesting. Their title doesn't have to be lofty. The office can be on the ground floor, with only one window. But the work must challenge their critical thinking skills and ignite a spark of enthusiasm. Boomers are crying out for work that doesn't bore them.

A recent AARP study found that 84 percent of workers in the Boomer generation would work even if they had no financial reason to do so (Singhania 2002). Fully 89 percent of the surveyed Boomers want work that "makes a contribution to society and helps people."

The retention options most often suggested by the Boomers in my interviews are:

❑ Flexible work schedules.

❑ Part-time job opportunities.

- ❏ Job-sharing options.
- ❏ Flexible benefits.
- ❏ Voluntary demotions.
- ❏ Active recruitment of older workers as company policy.
- ❏ Accommodations for employees with physical limitations.
- ❏ Longer vacation time.
- ❏ Training and development.

Even though training and development is listed last, it is by no means the least important retention option for companies to consider. In a recent article in *HR Magazine*, Robert Grossman cites a 2002 AARP survey of 1,500 workers aged 45 to 74 (Grossman 2003). Two thirds of this group said they want more leadership development and training. Unfortunately, two thirds of the executives in the surveyed companies in the same study indicated that leadership development is not consistently considered for older workers.

Training doesn't have to take the traditional form to be effective for Baby Boomer employees. Fortunately, options such as university distance learning and certificate courses are available. For instance, Xavier University in Cincinnati, Ohio, offers a Senior Management Certificate Program that brings senior managers up to date with the latest management technology but doesn't require the same length of time as a graduate degree. In her book *Age Works*, Beverly Goldberg suggests that companies should consider training bonuses for older employees, such as payment and/or time off for courses that teach new skills (Goldberg 2000).

According to the General Accounting Office, the proportion of workers age 55 and older is expected to increase by an average of 4 percent per year between now and 2015. The Bureau of Labor Statistics projects that workers in the 25–44 age group will decline to 44 percent of the workforce by 2008 (Dohm 2000). The numbers—and common sense—dictate that companies take proactive steps now towards retention of workers older than the age of 40.

Summary

If your organization wants to retain the best and the brightest of the Boomer generation, now is the time to tailor retention approaches to keep them engaged. Career advancement doesn't have to be linear, as it was early in this generation's career; however, this population wants to keep their minds active. They still want challenging assignments and lateral moves. As do the other generations, Boomers appreciate flexible hours and benefits. And they want one more thing: respect for the experience and expertise they bring to the workplace.

Case Study: Retaining Baby Boomers

Robert is frantic. He's the 32-year-old manager of the product development area of a 3-year-old software development company. A major product is about 90 percent complete and targeted for a marketing campaign next quarter. His problem? Susan, his 48-year-old lead software developer and client liaison, who has been with the company since day one, just announced that her husband is relocating to another state. They're leaving in three weeks.

Robert asked Susan if she'd stay with the company for the next six months and be available to finish developing and marketing the new product to major clients and potential clients across the United States and Canada. Susan had always been amenable to working long hours and traveling, so Robert was stunned when she said that her resignation would be effective in two weeks!

Susan, who has been married for 27 years, told Robert that she wants to support her husband in his new job. That would mean moving with him out of state and setting up a household so he could focus on work. Their two children are grown, not married, and live in two separate states. Susan plans to go back to work in her new location, but not for several months. Robert can understand why a person would leave for a better job—he has done that himself a time or two—but Susan's reasoning baffles him.

Questions for Discussion

1. What are the generational mindsets that might be operating in this case?
2. How can Robert entice Susan to stay with the organization?

Solution

Robert is a Gen Xer and Susan is a Baby Boomer, in terms of age. Robert, as many Xers do, completely understands moving from company to company to enhance one's career. He can even appreciate wanting to balance work and family life. He has difficulty understanding, however, why an ambitious, career-oriented person would leave an exciting job to do (in his mind) nothing. Susan was raised in a generation in which even career women often defer job decisions so their spouse can accept appealing and lucrative positions. Another frequent Boomer mindset is that women may work full-time but are primarily responsible for the home and child-rearing. In this scenario, Susan cannot imagine taking any steps that would be less than supportive of her husband.

Robert must act quickly to prevent critical expertise and experience from walking out the door. First, he needs to help Susan see how important she is to the team in product development and marketing. He can demonstrate this by telling her, of course, and also by providing a bonus or incentive for completing the project and a commission for product sales over the course of the first year. Robert could offer to let Susan telecommute from her new location and pay for a home office with appropriate technology. Part of the technology would be videoconference capability that would allow Susan to participate in sales pitches, in real time, from her home office. Lastly, Robert could reduce Susan's job to part-time for the short term but continue her benefit package. The short-term investment will pay off if the product is successfully launched and major clients are brought on board. If Robert can be flexible during Susan's transition, they both might discover that she could still easily work for the company even though she lives in a different state.

Chapter 7

Retaining Quality Gen Xers

Robin:

Remember in Chapter 3 when I described the background of a Gen Xer and concluded that we learned very early to be independent and fend for ourselves in order to survive? Survival is all about "me." So when you want to keep your Gen

Xers, you will need to be sure everything about your organization—from culture to benefits to policies—answers this question: "What's in it for me?"

From our research, there are five key areas—all of equal importance—that you should focus on in order to help retain your Gen Xers:

1. Company culture.
2. Management styles.
3. Work environment.
4. Career development.
5. Work–life balance.

Myth #5: Younger generations are not loyal

Gen Xers and Gen Ys feel it is a two-way street. If the company is loyal to them, they will be loyal in return—but cautiously. Both of these generations have grown up during times of the restructuring, downsizing, and layoffs of their parents, and now they're experiencing it themselves. One day they will be working beside someone, and the next day, with no warning, the person has been let go. As a result, Gen Xers' and Gen Ys' loyalties tend to be first to family, second to themselves, third to their community, fourth to their coworkers, and last to their employer. Employers who recognize and support these loyalties can actually *create* loyalty in their Gen X and Gen Y employees.

Company culture

No longer does anyone work for an organization for life or even long enough to get that gold pocket watch. Gen Xers learned about the disloyalty of employers the hard way when their parents were downsized and when prominent executives embezzled funds. They learned not to trust businesses.

To gain the trust and loyalty of a Gen Xer, you have to demonstrate that your business has values and integrity. This was one of the top three reasons why Gen Xers told us they stay with a business. You can't just preach that you do something; you've got to show them you do it. They need to understand your company's values and how you support them on a daily basis through the mission and vision and activities of the business. Plus, they need to see that your business is ethical and truly cares about your most important resource: the employees.

One sure way to help them understand that you care is by involving them. Gen Xers like the opportunity to provide input and make a contribution to the business. Find ways to involve them in the operations of the business and show them how what they are doing actually helps the business succeed. Then communicate, communicate, communicate. When employees hear about things firsthand from the organization, rather than from the grapevine or press, they will laud your integrity.

Management styles

One of the biggest reasons employees leave an organization is their supervisor. This is definitely true with Gen Xers. A supervisor must earn their respect and doesn't just get it by having the title "boss." Supervisors need to demonstrate that they understand the business and the employee's job thoroughly. They must be willing to roll up their sleeves and help the employee when needed.

Some key characteristics Gen Xers will look for in supervisors include someone who:

❏ Is approachable.

❏ Actively listens to their ideas, suggestions, and needs.

❏ Is supportive of their need for a life outside of work.

❏ Supports the values and goals of the organization.

❏ Has a high level of integrity.

❏ Provides regular and constant feedback beyond the annual review.

❏ Doesn't micro-manage but lets them do their job and ask for help if necessary.

❏ Provides credit for results through public recognition and/or rewards (such as time off, free lunch/dinner, tickets to a baseball game, movie passes).

❏ Encourages and supports employee growth and development.

Finally, their supervisor needs to be more than a boss...a mentor helping them continue to grow and succeed in their career and the company. If a Gen Xer isn't getting most of this from a supervisor, he or she will leave without hesitation and find it somewhere else.

Myth #6: Younger generations have no work ethic

What is work ethic? According to the Merriam-Webster Online Dictionary, "work ethic" is a belief in work as a moral good. And "moral" is defined as principles of right and wrong in behavior. So the real question becomes: What is right or wrong work behavior? I would guess each generation would give you a different definition. But I would also bet you that both generations have the same end goal in mind—meeting customer requirements in order to ensure the company's survival.

Both Gen Xers and Gen Ys feel they do have a strong work ethic towards ensuring the job is done and the company succeeds. However, their work ethic cannot be measured by when they come to work, how many hours they work, and how many breaks they take. Rather, these generations would like companies to measure their work ethic in terms of the results they produce—not how they do it, where they do it, or when they do it, as long as (necessary) deadlines are met.

Work environment

Work environment is also an important piece of the whole package that will help attract and retain Gen Xers in your workplace.

According to Linda Green Pierce from the consulting firm Northwest Legal Search, in her article "Gen X Change the Rules," the work environment needs to be family-like: "Companies...which create a home environment and home-like surroundings—a relaxed architectural setting, casual dress, the foosball table, the stocked refrigerator and peanut butter and crackers in the cupboard—create an environment where Xers will more readily stay on or stay to work late" (Pierce 2006).

Along with this family-like environment, it is also important to be sure the work environment is fun. Have you ever had an egg drop or turkey roll in the middle of the work day? At one of my clients' sites, to break up the stress of the office, everyone congregated in the lobby by the stairs and had an egg drop from the second floor to the first. It was one of many competitions between the men and women to keep the workplace fun. Or try this: Gregory Smith writes in his article "Baby Boomer versus Generation X" about the fun the staff at the Hyatt Regency in Lexington, Kentucky, had. They wrapped a large frozen turkey with electrical tape and then rolled it 50 feet toward the HR office trying to knock over wine bottle "bowling pins" (Smith 2005).

The types of things you do in your workplace to make it family-like and fun will vary greatly depending on your industry and company size. But there are many ways you can incorporate both attributes.

Some other strategies to incorporate into your work environment that appeal to Gen Xers include:

❑ Encouraging and welcoming new ideas and suggestions.

❑ Providing flexibility for Gen Xers to do their jobs the way they want as long as the appropriate end result is accomplished.

❑ Allowing them to juggle their schedule to finish their work and have a life outside work (such as compressed work week, early release on Fridays, or four 10-hour days).

❑ Creating a team-oriented atmosphere for accomplishing goals while still providing both individual and team recognition.

❑ Celebrating successes (for example, pitch-in lunch, happy hour, decorating the office).

❑ Creating a high-tech environment that uses state-of-the art technology, or at least not out dated technology.

Career development

The way to the heart of a Gen Xer is through career development and growth. When we surveyed 500 Gen Xers, more than 40 percent ranked career development opportunities as the number one reason that compels them to stay with an organization. Gen Xers want to grow and develop their skills to stay marketable in their profession. However, to do this you will need to use many different strategies to appeal to the needs of each employee—and you will definitely reap the benefits. Some suggestions include:

❑ Encourage the employee and manager to develop a career mission and detailed goals for accomplishing it.

❑ Provide opportunities for employees to learn through on-site and off-site training, job enrichment, job shadowing, college coursework, special projects, job rotations, and so on.

❑ Develop formal mentoring programs using the input of the participants to ensure it is beneficial for the mentor and mentee rather than a burden.

Additionally, we have found that Gen Xers like variety in their jobs. It helps them expand their skills and juggle multiple tasks simultaneously.

They are also technology thirsty. Having top, state-of-the-art technology expands their skills and helps them grow and keep pace with the improvements in technology. You'll be amazed at how much this will help your business.

Work–life balance

Generation Xers grew up watching both of their parents work long hours:

I never asked what was the best thing for me to do. I just kept working harder and eventually I hit what was right.

I never went home for dinner. Sure my kids missed me, but that's what it took in those days. (Pierce 2006)

Gen Xers aren't slackers and are definitely willing to do what it takes to get the job done and succeed in a company. But both men and women in this generation will *not* do it at the sacrifice of their "life," whether that is family or friends. For them, money is important, but it isn't the most important thing. Rather, a balance between money and the flexibility to enjoy life is most important to them. They will give up money for that balance any day.

For your organization to attract and retain Gen Xers, you will need to find out what will help them balance work and life. Remember that it is different for every individual, and this is a generation that is very individualistic. Some ideas include:

- ❏ Concierge services (for example, battery replacement on a watch, picking up a friend/relative at the airport, dinner on wheels, dry cleaning, oil change).
- ❏ Time off (paid or unpaid).
- ❏ Flexibility in core working hours (for example, comp time, late start or early end, snow days from home).
- ❏ Care packages for family during peak projects (for example, movie certificates, pizza coupons).
- ❏ On-site childcare and/or sick childcare.
- ❏ Encouraged involvement in children's activities (for example, school volunteering, coaching teams).
- ❏ Telecommuting.

More than anything, an organization with a management team that acknowledges that employees should have a life outside of work—and supports that need—will retain the brightest and the best Gen Xers. Remember: Other generations are quickly learning to ride the coattails of the Gen Xers' desire for a work–life balance. Implementing flexible work–life balance programs in your organization will help you retain not only Gen Xers, but employees in the other generations as well.

Summary

Tailor your benefit package, tailor your work hours, tailor rewards and recognition. "Tailor" is the word to summarize how to retain Gen Xers. This generation can be loyal—if an organization is willing to listen to their needs and not expect 24/7 employees. Xers will work diligently for managers they respect and for organizations that clearly contribute to their community. Xers have a work ethic. This work ethic may take a different form than that of previous generations, but if you win over an Xer, you'll have a dedicated, totally committed worker who will represent your mission and vision to the rest of the world.

Case Study: Promoting Younger Workers

Brad, a 25-year-old sales associate, recently applied for a promotion to expand his sales territory to include more prominent and critical accounts. When the sales director reviewed Brad's background in consideration for the position, she returned Brad's request to HR with a note saying he was too young. Her biggest concern was that Brad wasn't old enough to be knocking on the doors of customers who are primarily older. She didn't feel there was any way he would be able to gain credibility and respect with customers because he looks (and is) so young.

Questions for Discussion

1. Is age a bona fide requirement for this position?
2. What should you do to help the manager understand the value of the candidate?

Solution

The evaluation of a job candidate for a job, internal or external, should be based solely on the job requirements to avoid any discrimination claims. The law protects individuals ollder than 40, but a case of reverse discrimination could be attempted in the "sue-happy" society that we now live in.

The better approach for HR would be to focus on the job requirements and how Brad meets those requirements. Competency-based job descriptions are an excellent tool to help focus on *competencies* as opposed to *characteristics,* such as age, race, or gender. Because he is an internal candidate looking for a promotion, you have more information on his capabilities. It will be important to focus on his past performance, relationships, and credibility with customers, as well as knowledge of the company, products, and customers.

The sales director could also solicit input from current customers to determine how well Brad has done with them. Plus, the sales director could actually shadow Brad calling on an existing or even a new client to see how he would perform.

In this scenario, the sales director didn't take HR's advice and choose not to consider/promote Brad. Within a few months, Brad left the company for a sales position with the competition and rapidly became its top sales associate.

Chapter 8

Retaining Quality Gen Ys

Robin:

The best way to find out how to retain employees is to find out why they would leave. According to Chris Bailey in his article "Why Care About Generation Y?":

Data from the Full-time State Employee 2001 Turnover report indicates that 60 percent of turnover occurred with employees under the age of 40, and 52 percent of turnover was with employees that had less than two years of service. Why did they leave? Many employees felt their employer did not value their work, there was a lack of training, they were offered more responsibility elsewhere, they wanted to grow technologically, and they didn't feel recognized. (Bailey 2002)

Sounds very familiar, doesn't it? If we know these are reasons the younger generation is leaving or would consider leaving us, why don't we use the information to get them to stay? Here are some ways to help you retain Gen Ys that will even help you retain employees of other generations if you aren't careful.

Value their work. When we surveyed 500 Gen Ys, the number-one reason that compelled them to stay with a company was that their ideas/input were valued and respected. Gen Ys realize they are young and less experienced than the other generations and have a lot to learn. They are eager to learn, but at the same time they want to be adding value to the organization.

Myth #7: Younger generations are impatient

Who isn't impatient? The Gen Xers and Gen Ys are just the first generation to be bold enough to show it. Times have changed, including education, technology, the economy, and society. Old paradigms no longer work. The Gen Xers with technology skills and an average of about 10 years of work experience, combined with the Gen Ys with recent education and a lifetime of technology experience, are already making quality contributions and can make even more if the older generations are willing to accept them. But these younger generations aren't going to play by the "traditional" rules (such as going by seniority) unless a good reason is given. They are not going to wait five years to get the promotion just because that is the policy. If they have the skills and proven results to do the job, they expect the advancement, or they will go somewhere that will give it to them.

"Once employers talk values and give them meaningful roles in the company, they will engage Generation Y workers," stated Caela Farren in her article "Generation Y: A New Breed of Values and Desires" (Farren 2003). If you can get Gen Ys engaged by demonstrating that what they are doing is important to the success of the organization, you will motivate them to do their best and stay with you as long as they are adding value and contributing to the business. If you don't do this, you won't even be able to blink as fast as they will leave you for an organization promising—and delivering it.

Develop their career. Similar to the Gen Xers, the second-highest response we received from our surveyed Gen Ys was that career-development opportunities compel them to stay with an organization. They are very young in their careers and thirsty to learn and expand their skillset as much as possible.

There really isn't a "one size fits all" solution to providing career development opportunities to Gen Ys, though. Each Gen Y has his or her own individual needs. You'll need to identify what career development means to them and find ways to support those needs. Some examples include:

❑ Coaching.

❑ Mentoring.

❏ Job shadowing.

❏ Supporting role in a project.

❏ Job rotation.

❏ Training.

For Gen Ys, training needs to be highly interactive, utilizing technology to enhance learning. The training can come in many forms, from on-the-job to online to classroom.

The key is to meet with your Gen Ys and discuss their career goals and develop a career management plan that meets their needs. Assign a mentor to guide and support them in implementing their plan. Also, ensure their boss is a coach who will support and encourage them to fulfill their career goals as well.

Give them responsibility. This generation is very focused on improving themselves and thrives on responsibility. Caela Farren describes Gen Ys by saying, "This is clearly a do-it-yourself generation—likely to be the most entrepreneurial generation we have seen in decades" (Farren 2003). It shouldn't surprise us to know that, according to a survey published by the Adam Smith Institute, Britain's leading researcher and innovator of public services:

❏ Almost 50 percent of the Gen Y respondents said their career goal was to be a millionaire by 35.

❏ 48 percent want their own business.

Myth #8: Gen Ys can't add value

Too often, individuals in Generation Y have to fight being viewed as not having the years of experience to contribute anything to the company—which is a far cry from the truth. To begin with, this generation can run circles around the other generations in the workplace when it comes to technology. Almost every business decision is impacted by the rapid changes in technology today, and Gen Ys can make a huge contribution in that area. Plus, individuals in this generation are sponges, yearning to learn as much as they can and apply it immediately. Teach them what they need and let their fresh ideas find creative solutions to both the difficult and day-to-day issues of the business. Remember: Whether young or old, blue hair or gray, pierced or not, it's what's in the brains that adds value to the organization.

With all these ambitions and goals, this generation just needs to be given the responsibility to expand their skills base in order to be successful entrepreneurs and business owners in the very near future. Though this may worry you—that you may train them and then they'll leave—remember that they will be more loyal to you because you are providing this skill to them, and they may actually become an *intrapreneur* and help your business grow. In addition, it is likely these individuals may be the ones who will run your organization in 10–20 years. So some ways to give them responsibility include:

❏ Allowing them to do a project their way as long as the end result meets the project needs.

❏ Providing them with multiple challenging assignments to manage at the same time with little guidance.

❏ Giving them an opportunity to be an active participant/partner on a team.

❏ Setting clear expectations for them and explaining "why" they need to do something (then backing off and letting them do the work and seek direction when needed).

❏ Allowing them to have the opportunity to actively get to know the business and what it takes for a business to succeed.

These methods will help them feel ownership and responsibility for their assignments, grow their business skills, and add value to the organization. This is what they love and will stick around to continue to receive.

Utilize technology. Bruce Tulgan of Rainmaker Thinking, a 14-year-old company that researches generational dynamics in the workplace, said it best in his article "Managing the Generation Mix—Part II" when he stated, "keep Yers focused with speed, customization, and interactivity" (Tulgan 2002). This generation was raised with the birth of the Internet and knows that any business can be found at *www.*... Many of them probably started on a computer as a toddler and have had their own Web page since their pre-teen years. So "companies that aren't technically savvy are not going to get these employees to work for them," says Chris Bailey (Bailey 2002).

Your organization must utilize technology as an integral part of the day-to-day operations of the business. You need to be sure your employees have the technical tools they need to do their jobs right. You definitely do not want to have outdated and obsolete systems and software.

Provide recognition. Gen Ys grew up playing the variety of video games flooding the markets, such as Nintendo, PlayStation, and computer games. Far from being mere entertainment, these games have helped establish their work styles. Gen Ys are used to:

❏ Having very clear expectations of what they need to do.

❏ Receiving continuous assessments on where they stand.

❏ Obtaining constant feedback.

Given this, it isn't surprising to hear that receiving feedback and recognition for their performance is very important to them. Your organization will need to help managers learn that this generation needs more frequent recognition and feedback than the annual performance review. Recognition could include:

❑ Publicly recognizing the employee for his or her efforts.

❑ Writing a note to the employee.

❑ Personally thanking the employee for his or her efforts.

❑ Providing (even small) rewards (such as company-logo shirts, lunch with the CEO, Starbucks dollars, afternoon off, or tickets to an event).

"Studies have shown that the top motivating techniques are those initiated by the manager and based on employee performance," explained Carol Hacker in her article "Recruiting and Retaining Generation Y and X Employees" (Hacker 2003). The manager is the key to ensuring your employees are receiving the recognition they deserve for their performance. Be sure you have trained them and provided them with the resources to give this recognition.

Beyond mastering these five key areas to ensure you are retaining your Gen Ys, there are a few other things you can also consider. As do the Gen Xers, this generation looks for a company that offers a fun and family-like work environment. They too would give up pay in return for time to have a life. So the inclusion of flexible policies with regard to when and where to be at work are definitely seen as a retention tool by Gen Ys.

Finally, this generation seeks security and safety from their employers. This can take many forms, from reassuring them of the stability of their job to taking care of them no matter what the circumstances may be (recessed economy, loss of a major client). Do you discuss how you are preparing for or preventing these downturns from impacting your employees? Are you providing the proper checks and balances to ensure the organization is operating with the highest level of integrity? What measures are you taking to provide safety for your employees? How will your organization handle an Anthrax scare, a natural disaster, a bomb threat, or even workplace violence? Are you communicating these disaster plans?

Yes, this generation is young and has a lot to learn. But we were in their shoes once. These are the future employees, managers, and leaders of our organizations. Let's do what we can to ensure we are retaining and developing them.

Summary

Gen Y is similar to previous generations in one key characteristic: They want to be treated with respect. They want to make significant contributions to their organizations as they learn; not wait 10–15 years to "pay their dues." If Gen Y can be provided with challenging career development opportunities as they learn their current job, there's a high likelihood of retention. This generation doesn't want parents in the workplace. They want the opportunity to receive clear expectations from employers, and then find their own path towards achieving positive results to meet those expectations.

Case Study: Gen Y Work Ethic

You're the HR manager at Savings 'R' Us Bank, located in the Midwest. One of the summer interns, a college sophomore, has received his fifth complaint in as many days from coworkers about his "poor work ethic." Complaints have ranged from "he saunters in 10 minutes late every day" to "he's on his cell phone when he should be answering the bank's phone." This is only the intern's second week, and you already spoke to him after his third day to direct him to follow written guidelines for each assigned task, be prompt and on time, and speak respectfully to his coworkers. The intern still hasn't met these expectations.

Questions for Discussion

1. Should you just "cut your losses" and fire the intern?

2. How can you ensure the experience for the next two months is a positive one if you decide not to fire him?

Solution

In this scenario, there's a specific organizational culture—a bank. Even though banks have tried to be more "outgoing" in terms of organizational personality over the last decade, banks still attract more people who are interested in finance and accounting, details, and transaction interaction rather than people interaction. Additionally, there's a geographic culture in that the bank is located in the Midwest, which usually is more conservative and traditional than some other areas of the Ununted States. Besides these two factors, there are different generations with various notions of the term "work ethic" within the same organization. The easy answer is to cut your losses and fire the intern. The better answer is that there are probably some actions that can be taken to salvage the situation. Summer interns and temporary employees can potentially make excellent long-term employees, so the effort is likely to be worthwhile.

The intern is a college sophomore and probably in his early 20s: a Generation Y employee. He has very likely grown up with peers that are casual as opposed to formal. He is accustomed to older adults proving themselves to him before he respects them, as opposed to affording people respect solely based on their age, title, or years of service.

The complaints should be investigated on more than a superficial level. Does he really come in past his scheduled work time, or do older workers typically clock in early (and expect others to do the same)? If he is indeed coming in late, this "Gen Why-er" should be told not only that there is a certain time he must be ready to start work but *why* he must be available at the designated time. When he understands how her work is connected with meeting customer needs, he may be punctual. The same holds true for the written guidelines for her assigned tasks. It would be more helpful and meaningful if his trainer told him *why* he was doing each task. Is the intern's first responsibility to answer the phone? If it is, then by all means he should be instructed as to the policy on responding to incoming calls. Or maybe it's a work culture in which anyone who's handy picks up a ringing phone, regardless of job duties. This is an example of a different "work ethic" and needs to be addressed among the department employees.

Many Gen Y employees have benefited from being assigned a mentor to help them understand organizational culture and "the way things are done"—and why. This is an option that could be helpful in the case of summer interns and new hires.

Chapter 9

Get Ready, 'Cause Here I Come

Linda and Robin:

The Millennials, also referred to by sociologists as Generation 9-11, will be making their way into the workforce within the next five years. For this reason, we felt it was important to provide some research and information on this generation as employers begin to prepare to bring them into the workplace. Some authors use the term "Millennials" to refer to Generation Y, but we believe that technological and other changes in the world have been and will be so rapid and have such a strong impact that there is a marked difference in the motivations and choices young people do and will make, starting with those born in 1991—our Millennials.

The oldest members of this generation were born in a time when more parents in our country were focused on children first than in any previous generation. The parents also found themselves having to shelter those children to protect them from the harms of the world—drugs, child abductions, school shootings, bombings....

The Millennials generation is being raised as the center of their universe, basking in adult attention, praise, and protection within their families. We found the young people we interviewed in this age group to be confident, happy, and secure.

As they enter the workforce, employers will need to understand that the Millennials are techno-savvy to an extremely high degree. Remember that the World Wide Web was officially released in 1991, quite symbolic of this generation. According to a study by the Pew Internet and American Life Project:

❑ 87 percent of U.S. teens use the Internet.

❑ 51 percent go online each month.

❑ 45 percent own a cell phone.

❑ 89 percent use e-mail (but most prefer to use instant messaging).

❑ 32 percent use IM every day.

In focus group discussions during this study, the teens revealed that they use e-mail as a means to talk to "old people"; otherwise, instant messaging is the mode of communication (Lenhart 2005).

We've found that young teens today care for one another and build communities in their classrooms and neighborhoods alike. They are not callous. They are not disengaged. Instead, the teens we've observed and interviewed want to please others, are spiritual, and are looking forward to making lifelong contributions to the world. If Gen Xers were the lost generation, the Millennials are the found generation.

We discovered in our interviews a generation of young teens who are patriotic and believe our country must stay strong and united in the aftermath of September 11th. They trust authority figures at school that monitor their comings and goings, use Web cams to follow their activities, and conduct locker checks. After the Columbine shootings in 1999, this lack of privacy is seen as acceptable for the 15-years-and-younger students we talked with. They see monitoring by adults as a means of protection for them.

This is a generation that is, as Gen Y was before them, very willing to engage in community service activities such as Habitat for Humanity, soup kitchens, and homeless shelters. Many of them told us that they view Gen Xers as selfish and self-absorbed, and they want to be selfless and contribute to the world around them. This is a good thing, becausethe Gen Ys we interviewed indicated that they would expect community service and outreach of their co-workers and direct reports once they enter the management ranks.

We've found that members of this youngest generation are willing to be team players. They are being encouraged at a young age to get along with everyone and accept differences. They have more activities to get involved in than any other generation, and many of those are team sports, which are teaching Millennials at a young age how to work with others effectively, whether they're male or female. This is also the generation for whom it is not uncommon for a team to be co-ed, with all players being of equal contribution and skill.

Implications for the workplace

In 2007, the oldest Millennials will be 16 and starting their first forays into the workforce. The steps employers are already putting into place to attract and retain Gen Ys will serve them well for this next generation too.

If you provide time off (with pay) for employees to engage in community and civic volunteer activities, keep doing that. If you provide flexible hours for appropriate positions and the opportunity to telecommute, keep doing that. If you provide concierge services, keep doing that. As with the other generations, ask these younger employees what types of services would help them. Dry cleaning and car washes may not be as important to them as nearby or on-site lattes. But more importantly, the Millennials will really be looking for an atmosphere that is friendly, fun, and safe.

As with the Gen Ys before them, the Millennials may not have confrontational skills for effective interactions with coworkers and customers. Plan to continue your professional development activities for this generation and include teambuilding, negotiating, and conflict-resolution skills.

Technology will be more critical for this generation than any before. They've grown up with at least one, two, and sometimes more computers in their homes. PCs have always had flat monitors—or so they will tell you. Most of their games have been electronic, from handhelds (such as Nintendo's Game Boy) to the PC (such as the *Tycoon* series, *Pajama Sam*, and *Rise of Nations*) to consoles (such as the PlayStation, GameCube, and Xbox). They've even had electronic pets (such as Tamagotchi and Furbys) and virtual online pets (such as Webkinz). Without state-of-the-art technology in your workplace, they will be lost— and will seek it elsewhere.

This is a confident generation that will want and expect challenge and opportunity on the job—immediately. You can't necessarily give every incoming employee the position of vice president, but you can provide short-term assignments that they can spearhead and for which they can receive immediate feedback. Help them feel that they "own" parts of their work and assignments and they'll be very productive for your organization.

Feedback with this generation will be even more critical than the Gen Xers and Gen Ys before them. They've grown up with instant feedback and praise from parents, teachers, and interactive games. They are used to receiving a reward and recognition for nearly anything they do— a sticker for a job well done, a piece of candy for cooperating. Just because they've grown up doesn't mean their minds have been de-trained to expect this same instant feedback, recognition, and reward.

The Millennials we've interviewed and observed find it cool to be identified as a smart kid, whereas in previous generations it was definitely *not* cool to be seen as smart. The young people we interviewed enjoy school and look forward to going on to college and graduate school. That bodes well for the workplace of 2020.

As an employer committed to our future workforce, you need to engage yourself in their continued education. The skills we will need in the future are unimaginable. We need to partner with this younger generation and their educational institutions to ensure they do have the motivation—and the finances—to continue their education. And we need to ensure we are providing the academic institutions with financial support and input on what the students need to learn to be productive and successful in the future workplace.

For most everyone in the workforce, with the exception of a few young Gen Ys, the Millennial generation is hard to imagine, let alone try to relate to and accommodate in the workplace. This generation was raised primarily by Baby Boomers and Gen Xers (and technology), so that is why they believe as they do. We'll need to understand them because we need them in the workplace and can learn a great deal from them.

Summary

Millennials will continue the push that began with Gen Xers for cutting-edge technology in the workplace. They will continue to encourage their employers to provide paid time off for them to engage in community activities, just as the Gen Ys before them. From the employer's standpoint, you will want to continue professional development to help young employees build conflict resolution and verbal communications skills. Just as the generations before them we've written about in this book, Millennials expect to be respected and recognized as the unique individuals they are.

Case Study: Retaining Millennials

Becky is the proud owner of a trendy boutique that specializes in jeans and jewelry for pre- to late-teen girls. Becky, who's right out of undergraduate school herself, used an inheritance to open her store. She's not a 9-to-5 kind of girl, so she thinks this is a smart career move—except for one problem: keeping sales staff!

Becky can't have people in their 30s and 40s selling to young girls. She hires teenagers who are 16 or 17 who want a little extra spending money or who are saving for college. The girls she hires are gone practically as soon as they start! Or worse yet, they don't show up for work if they have a little headache or had a fight the night before with their boyfriends. The last sales clerk left because a customer was "rude" to her. Becky was amazed. The customer simply said she didn't like the employee's suggestion for a shirt for her daughter. Becky can't keep her store running efficiently without sales staff, especially on weekends. She hates the idea that she may have to close the store, but it's a real possibility.

Question for Discussion

1. What steps can Becky take to find employees who will (a) show up and (b) stay with her for at least a few months?

Solution

In the interview process, Becky should include some time for applicants to observe her interaction with customers. This could be in real time or on videotape. Applicants could then see the level of customer service expected and understand what the job entails. In the on-boarding process for new sales associates, Becky could provide training on customer interactions. This might be as simple as role-plays that demonstrate how to handle different personalities they often encounter.

Incentives work across all age groups. Becky could offer merchandise as sales bonuses (name brands please!). She might offer retention bonuses after one month, two months, and so on. Cash incentives might also be effective, to allow employees to choose how they want to invest their extra money. Becky could consider using her sales staff as models for TV or print ads, to provide them with "bragging rights" or the start of a portfolio if they're interested in modeling as a career.

To entice your younger employees to show up when they should and stay with the organization, tailor rewards and recognition to their interests. When in doubt, consider cash!

Chapter 10

Managing Conflict Across Generations

Sources of generational conflict

Linda and Robin:

In a recent survey conducted by the Society for Human Resource Management, 40 percent of human resource professionals have observed conflict among employees as a direct result of generational differences! In organizations with 500 or more employees, 58 percent of HR professionals reported conflict between younger and older workers, largely due to differing perspectives on work ethic and work–life balance. This data tells us that there's a huge potential for miscommunication, low morale, and poor productivity—unless the generations figure out the sources of conflict and learn how to handle them successfully.

The largest source of conflict is the debate about work ethic. The Radio Baby generation worked hard out of necessity because of the Great Depression and men being away fighting WWII, leaving women to fill demanding factory positions. This generation taught its children, the Baby Boomers, the meaning of sacrifice and "climbing the ladder" to success by "paying your dues." Small wonder then that members of these two generations aren't totally receptive to the suggestion by younger employees that work hours, work rules, and work methods should be open to discussion. In the minds of many older employees, there *is* no discussion. But younger employees have learned by watching their parents and grandparents that they need to have control of their work schedules, while at the same time fully agree that the quality and result shouldn't be negatively impacted.

In order to help the different generations in the workplace handle this conflict, the recommendation we make to managers is to consider the *results,* or objectives, rather than the *process* of reaching those results. If a job lends itself to telecommuting, why not expand the pool of employees who may be interested in that job by providing that option? Technology allows Internet and phone communication between customers and employees to appear seamless, and what the customers really want is answers and assistance, not the knowledge that the person helping them is sitting behind a desk in a downtown office. We are not suggesting, however, that work quality be compromised in any way. If most customers of an organization have made it clear that they want to have "live" access to staff—in person—as early as 8 a.m., then employees need to be accessible at 8 a.m., and ready to provide a quality service. The Gen Ys, however, will want to know why this is necessary instead of being abruptly told "this is the way it is."

The second-largest source of conflict is the demand of the younger generations for work and family balance. Again, the younger generations grew up with both parents working resulting in very little "family time." The older generations see this demand for work–life balance as another example of the poor work ethic of the younger generations. Adding more fuel to this fire, employers try to meet the needs of a good work–life balance but don't consider the needs of everyone, and then conflict becomes very apparent.

To avoid and/or minimize the conflict, an organization needs to have options and benefits available to *all* employees that help make their balance between work and family life amiable. However, if work and family balance options only provide balance for young parents between 25 and 30, certainly other segments of the workforce will be frustrated and conflict will result.

Work ethic and work–life balance are just two sources of conflict among the generations. There are so many differences between the generations that we've discussed in this book, and with any difference conflict can result if an effort isn't made to understand and respect the difference. Minimizing and avoiding conflict begins by recognizing the source of the conflict—work ethic, work–life balance, "putting in their time," loyalty, respect, career options, technology, educational opportunities, or dress code. Each generation will respond to conflict in different ways. Recognizing that response, determining the source, and handling the conflict appropriately will always end in a positive outcome.

Responses to conflict

Linda's mother worked as a nurse for the local hospital in her home town for almost 30 years. There were many times when she, or her peers, disagreed with nurse supervisors or hospital administrators. She would express her frustration to Linda, and in turn Linda (as a Baby Boomer) would always suggest that she respectfully bring these concerns to the attention of those in leadership positions. Her reply? "Oh no...they're the bosses. I couldn't do that!" We've heard similar stories from other members of the Radio Baby generation. They tend to respect authority (even if they don't necessarily agree with or even respect the particular individual in the position). Confronting a person in a supervisory position is not the method of choice among Radio Babies for dealing with conflict.

Baby Boomers are more likely to respond to potential conflict by saying, "Let's bring the team together and we'll resolve this." Perhaps the person in the top leadership role will make a decision on the final disposition of an issue, but there's probably going to be some input from everyone involved.

Along come the Gen Xers: independent, individualistic, clear on what they want to achieve in the workplace. They will largely ignore older coworkers' efforts to "tell them what to do" or parent them. They will tell their coworkers in a straightforward way if there's something they disagree with or don't like. And according to the Gen Ys in the workplace, there's a lot the Xers don't like!

Generation Y likes to take a more casual, relaxed approach to the workplace. They enjoy a friendly atmosphere and calling coworkers—and customers for that matter—by their first names. This is a generation that doesn't cope well with "in your face" conflict, such as unhappy customers complaining curtly about service. Coaching on confronting issues (and people) in a positive and assertive way is definitely necessary for many in this generation.

Providing constructive feedback

There are certainly some generally accepted, effective ways for giving constructive criticism and feedback that will minimize conflict. Additionally, some approaches work best for older employees; others for younger generations. This is another one of those cases in which one size does not fit all.

In all cases, remember these key points for offering constructive criticism:

Focus on the issue. Stay away from personality attacks and peripheral issues, and simply hone in on the problem or concern under discussion. Don't jump all over the place or let the other person distract you from the subject. The subject should be work-focused, not personal.

Emphasize key points. There are probably two or three key points that are critical to the discussion. Be clear and precise with those points so they're not buried under less important details.

Be specific about what you think or want.
Lead with your concern or main point, then let the
other person know exactly what needs to change
and why.

Acknowledge the other's point of view. Whether
or not you agree with another's point of view, he or
she has a right to say why he believes or act as he
does. You're more likely to change his mind, or his
behavior, if you understand what compels that
behavior.

Avoid "hot button" language. Stay away from
name-calling or using demeaning words. Maintain
your dignity and help preserve the other person's
as well.

Based on our interviews with members of each generation, as well as our own life experiences, we have some
suggestions for providing constructive feedback across
generations.

Radio Babies

Express appreciation for their efforts. Acknowledge that
they have the interests of their department/organization
at heart. Let them know how changes in their behavior will
increase their value to the organization.

Baby Boomers

Emphasize the need for their input into team success.
Discuss an action plan together for improving their skills
or changing behaviors.

Gen Xers

Be straightforward. Be honest. Focus on results expected, and offer tools and techniques to help them ac-
quire knowledge or skills. Don't start any conversation with,
"Back in my day...."

Gen Ys

Emphasize business reasons for any changes you ask them to make. Explain how what they do, or don't do, affects the company's viability. Let them know you're there to help and will touch base with them on how they're doing—and soon.

Turning conflict into collaboration: tactics that provide positive results

The most successful tactic you'll ever use to get positive results from initial conflict is to help identify what the business problem is and call on people involved to attack the problem, not each other. For example:

A 40-year-old male department head in an organization was frustrated because one of his direct reports, a 25-year-old woman, seemed to ignore his orders and "do things her own way." The department head didn't like having his authority undermined because he'd worked for 15 years to get to his position. The woman who was his direct report joined the company within the previous year and had experience with other work methods that she felt provided equally effective results. If she disagreed with her boss (or anyone else), she would say so. They were at an impasse, and the young woman was ready to quit when they called Linda in.

Instead of starting off by asking them, "What's your problem?" Linda asked them about the mission of the company and the objectives of their department. Interestingly, this conversation surfaced one important fact. They both agreed on the mission and vision of the organization, as well as the primary objectives of the department! And they were clearly surprised that they were in agreement. Then Linda asked them both what their customers wanted and how they knew if customer needs were met. Again, they both had the same thoughts about what their customers wanted and the level of quality necessary to satisfy customer demands. Again, they were both surprised.

By this time, they were loosening up about the process for getting results. The department head could see that his employee had the interests of the company and their customers in mind when doing her work. The direct report could see the same with her boss. Linda left them by asking them to discuss suggestions they each had to enhance the product and services they provided. They were deeply involved in a constructive conversation when she left.

Summary

Generational differences increase an organization's vulnerability to miscommunication, misunderstanding, and unproductive conflict. Organizations that resolve potential conflicts effectively have learned to focus on results, as opposed to zooming in on traditional ways of getting those results. Generation Y in particular is turned off by negative criticism and high levels of stress. They want a "kinder, gentler" workplace. Even though each generation has learned to deal with conflict in different ways, some commonalities of strategy do exist:

❏ Listen to the other's point of view.

❏ Acknowledge the other person's right to have a point of view.

❏ Focus on organizational goals and objectives— listen as an ally to strategize for success.

Case Study: Managing Conflict

A manager of a group of 15 employees spanning all four generations comes to you, the human resources rep, with a problem. Some of the older workers are complaining that the younger employees are playing computer games over lunch. They feel this is inappropriate behavior on the job; the younger generations say that it is relaxing to them, and who cares what they do for their lunch time?

Question for Discussion

1. How should you coach the manager to handle this conflict between her employees?

Solution

Before coaching the manager on this situation, the HR person needs to do a little homework:

1. What is the established company policy regarding personal use of company computers? If there is a policy against the use of company computers for personal use including games, then the procedure in the policy should be followed, and followed consistently across all employees.

2. Are the games the employees are playing offensive or causing harassment to others? If so, the company policy regarding harassment should be followed.

3. Are the games the employees are playing distracting others from doing their jobs? If so, the manager will want to address the issue from a productivity perspective.

If the answer to these three questions is no, the HR person should coach the manager to talk to both groups further about the issue. If the manager isn't comfortable having the conversation, then HR may need to do it. For the employees with the complaint, find out what impact the game-playing is having on them. Depending on the response, explain to them that there is no policy prohibiting this action, and ask them what they do during their lunch breaks. Explain that the other employees have chosen to spend their lunches playing the games in order to relax and be more productive when their break is over.

The manager will also need to talk to the younger employees. To begin with, they may not even be aware that there is a problem. Be sure they understand what the company policy is regarding using company equipment and time for personal use. Ask them to be sure that what they are playing is not distracting or offensive to others. Also, they may want to consider including others in their games.

Chapter 11

Older Workers, Younger Bosses

Part I: How to work for a younger boss

Linda:

It had to happen at some point. As we spend more years in the workplace, it's inevitable that you will eventually report to someone younger than yourself. When that time came for my friend

John, however, it was a jolt! He was 42 and his new boss was (gasp!) 29. That's a generation—and a world—apart.

John had been in his position as a mid-level manager at a large manufacturing company for five years and in his field for 20. He believed that he'd been around the block and knew the ropes. The new boss was brought in from the company that acquired his, and he was already at a director level. Ouch.

John had only been working with his new boss for about three months when he called me, furious, with this complaint: "This kid isn't even wet behind the ears yet and she thinks she knows everything! So she has an MBA from an Ivy League school—I have a bachelor's degree and several other degrees from the School of Hard Knocks." John had heard from his boss the phrase, "This is the way I learned to handle this situation at Wharton," one too many times that day.

I asked John if he wanted to continue working with the organization, younger boss or not. He thought a moment and then indicated that he most certainly did, especially in light of its excellent compensation package and the fact that he has two children in college. In order to help John, and many similar to him in the Baby Boomer or Radio Baby generation, I developed these suggestions for working with a boss younger than yourself:

Tip #1: Your boss doesn't want a parent

You won't score any points by approaching a younger boss as a protective parent. As a matter of fact, this generation has a name for parents or pseudo-parents who hover: helicopter parents. It is not a term of endearment.

It's an interesting dichotomy. Gen X and Gen Y interviewees told me they want a family-type atmosphere at work, but they *don't* want coworkers or managers acting as their mom or dad. Gen Ys especially want a collegial workplace in which they are comfortable talking about work or personal issues with the CEO, peers, and direct reports. Friendliness they want. A family atmosphere they want. Mom and Dad as their direct report—they don't want.

Tip #2: Your boss wants you to listen

I mean *really* listen—engage those active listening skills you learned back in your first supervisory workshop. Dust them off and put them to use with the younger boss. If the boss is a Gen Xer, he or she is likely to be very engaged and involved with your organization's core values. His or her ideas and approach will directly relate to those values. The younger boss will be intent upon ensuring that his or her actions, and those of her direct reports, reflect the mission, vision, and values of the company. When the younger boss shares perspectives on achieving the business objectives, he or she is serious. A lot of thought has gone into the perspectives offered. Even if you disagree, listen attentively and don't discount suggestions immediately with statements such as, "We've done that before, and it didn't work."

Tip #3: Expect a laid-back management style

The Gen Xer supervisors I interviewed said that a big source of discomfort with their older direct reports is the amount of hands-on supervision requested. Surprisingly, the Gen Xer managers indicated they'd like to "back off" their direct reports and just focus on end results. Often, the older workers said they'd like to have more direction and input along the way. Baby Boomers especially told me that they prefer decision-making as a team effort, but their boss was more comfortable with direct reports working autonomously and then sharing their results.

If you are a Baby Boomer or Radio Baby, consider sending e-mail updates to the boss periodically, just so you have a paper trail to satisfy your need to commit activities to writing, and the boss receives some input he or she can read or store for future reference. You can of course request face-to-face meetings when an issue requires that richness of communication; however, I suggest you also get comfortable with leaving voice messages and e-mail follow-up messages.

Tip #4: Do NOT call the boss after hours

Your boss may not yet have a family; however, that doesn't mean he or she does not value personal time away from the office. If the office closes as 5 p.m., it's very likely that your boss will be leaving within a short time afterwards. The boss has a life to live and fully expects that the job will not interfere with it!

If the office opens at 8 a.m., don't look for the boss at 7:30. If the boss gives you his or her cell phone number and asks you to call outside work hours with *critical* questions or issues, then by all means take advantage of that offer. Get proficient with sending e-mails or leaving voice messages as well (see the previous section).

Tip #5: Demonstrate your reliability early and often

The Gen X or Gen Y boss will not be particularly impressed with your years of experience or the degree you earned 10 years ago. You'll need to demonstrate your current skills and competencies as they relate to the department's mission, vision, and objectives. In other words, the younger boss wants to know "what have you done for us lately?"

This is the primary recommendation I made for my friend John mentioned earlier in this chapter. If you've had successful, profitable ideas and job enhancements within the past year, make sure that's what you share with the boss. If he or she has a pet project or approach, think of ways to make it work (as opposed to reasons it won't work). Or if the idea simply is unrealistic, you can offer alternatives...as a colleague rather than the "voice of wisdom."

The younger boss wants mentors. Demonstrate how you can help him or her be a hero and you will find that the boss comes to you more and more often. Then you won't have to pursue the boss to offer your suggestions.

Tip #6: Talk the talk

No, I don't mean that you have to learn Gen Y slang (although that couldn't hurt). You will need to pursue a careful balance between understanding age appropriate jargon and using it, however. I have observed that Gen Ys feel that older people are being condescending when they overuse "their" pet phrases.

When I suggest you "talk the talk," I mean that you should be aware of the media influences in the younger person's world. If you occasionally read the same periodicals, listen to the same radio talk shows and the same music, you're more likely to understand what topics appeal to this age group. Then you can provide analogies and ideas that grab their attention. Don't know where to start? Here are some suggestions:

One of the "hot" periodicals for Generation X is *Fast Company*. And the most recommended Websites for Gen Ys are:

❑ *www.ypulse.com* (daily news and commentary).

❑ *www.myspace.com* (Internet community).

❑ *www.generationwhy.com* (written by a Gen Y for Gen Ys).

❑ *www.millennialsrising.com* (written by Neil Howe and William Strauss, co-authors of *Generations*).

Some of the typical TV shows that Gen Xers and Gen Ys told us they watched are:

❑ *The O.C.*

❑ *Lost.*

❑ *Punk'd.*

❑ *South Park.*

❑ *The Apprentice.*

❑ *Survivor.*

❑ *Alias.*

❑ *24.*

Likewise, some of the more popular movies with these younger generations were said to be:

❑ The *Lord of the Rings* trilogy.

❑ The *Harry Potter* series.

❑ *Pulp Fiction.*

❑ *Kill Bill.*

❑ The *Star Wars* series.

Now that you've heard my perspective as a Boomer, I think it only fair that you hear from a Gen Xer about the same subject from the other side—working with older direct reports.

Part II: How to manage older direct reports

Robin:

The classic example of the young boss managing older direct reports can be seen in the movie *In Good Company*. In this movie, Dennis Quaid plays the "pre-historic dinosaur," a

51-year-old who ultimately reports to Topher Grace, the overly confident 26-year-old new boss. Though the movie is meant to be a comedy, it actually hits home for many more than you would think.

Topher Grace starts his first day as the new boss professing to a strange girl on the elevator that he is "scared shitless" and proceeds into the board room filled with about 10 grande lattes to meet his new team. Not prepared, he fumbles through the meeting and ends by copying the sentiments of the owner of the company, "Teddy K": It's all about synergy and having fun! I won't ruin the rest of the movie for you, but I will use its ideas to help develop the lessons learned for how to manage older direct reports.

Tip #1: Make the right impression

Do you want to be the boss because you need a few minutes of fame or because you feel qualified with a vested interest? If it is for a moment of fame, please spare the rest of the younger generations the humiliation and get fame another way. To "be the boss" does not mean come in being bossy, but rather setting the example for others.

To begin with, your first impression is absolutely crucial. You do not get a second chance to make a first impression. Although it may seem superficial, you need to dress the part. If you are the boss, you should be dressed one step up from everyone else, which means no sandals, T-shirts, raggedy jeans, piercings, unnatural hair color, or skin-showing. Dress to impress (but don't *over*-impress).

Be prepared—as in, have a plan, and do not show up so filled with caffeine that you can't function. Really get to know what your job will be and who the individuals are who will be working on your team (such as roles, tenure, strengths). Also prepare how you are going to present yourself to the team.

Will it be one on one or as a group? The answer depends on which way you can best convey that you are confident in your abilities to be the boss without coming across as arrogant and immature.

Tip #2: Don't try to make a 50-year-old think the way you do

Although you may think 50-plus-year-olds are "prehistoric dinosaurs," you don't need to make them feel that way. You need to lose the slang (for example, "word," "LOL," "awesome") in the workplace so everyone is on the same page. Slang only frustrates and/or intimidates older workers and definitely does not gain their respect. Think about it—how do you feel when they make a statement about something or someone that was "before your time"? It's very awkward! But on that same note, when they do make statements that were "before your time," learn from them; don't blow them off or disrespect them by making them feel "old." For example, just as we do not like to be told that they have "underwear older than us," they don't like to be told they are as old or older than our parents.

Remember, as we explained in Chapter 2, that each generation grew up with different societal, social, and economic issues. Plus, members of each generation are at a different point in their lives; therefore, values are very different. For a Gen Y, time with friends on a Sunday afternoon may be just the ticket but for a Baby Boomer time with family is priceless. Try to keep a frame of reference for how your values and lifestyle may differ from that of older workers working for you, and don't try to make their lives change to mirror yours.

Tip #3: Listen to the guidance of mature employees

One very positive strength the older generations have on us younger generations is *experience*. We don't need to re-invent the wheel or make mistakes that have already been made. So use your teams (Baby Boomers especially like this) for brainstorming and creating solutions. The older generations are not trying to knock down your ideas, but rather they have a good reason for why they do things a certain way. Listen to their reasons and show respect for their experience and expertise. Together you can learn from their reasons and integrate your ideas to come up with an even better solution.

In *In Good Company*, Dennis Quaid is a successful sales manager because he really gets to know his clients—personal facts, ways to approach, and so on. Topher Grace doesn't take the time to listen to Dennis Quaid explain why he does this. At one point, Topher vetoed an outing to a basketball game and instead took the clients to a hot new rock concert, which would have been great if the clients weren't 50-plus too, and had no interest in a loud rock concert.

People in an older generation may appear "stuck in their ways," but it behooves us to listen and try to understand the reason behind their position. There are always at least two ways to skin a cat.

Tip #4: Do not lower requirements or expectations

Oftentimes, the stereotype is that older workers are not capable of doing the same level of work as younger employees. This is so not true. In our research, older workers insisted they didn't want to be treated as though they were less intelligent or less able to contribute. From an employer standpoint, customers will be lost and productivity will suffer if *any* employee is allowed to work at a level lower than standard (regardless of age). Younger bosses need to be sure they don't get caught lowering the requirements or expectations of older workers. This will cause friction and impact the output of the organization.

Tip #5: Don't make assumptions

The old saying that "old dogs can't learn new tricks" is far from the truth. First of all, is 51 really "old"? Folks are living much longer than they ever have due to advances in healthcare, which means 60 really could be the new 40. When we interviewed the older generations, both Radio Babies and Baby Boomers were looking for jobs that gave them an opportunity to grow and learn new things. They told us "old dogs" *can* and *want* to learn new tricks, and their brains are still working, so don't treat them as though they're not. In other words, as a young boss, don't assume your older workers can't or don't want to learn something new.

For example, technology is changing very rapidly, and most assume the older generations can't keep up. When visiting one of my clients recently, their IT guru—who knew more than I did about computers—was a 60-plus-year-old woman. Often, I find myself coaching family and friends in the older generations on technologies such as computers, cell phones, and PDAs. Most of this comes naturally to the younger generations because we grew up with it always being there. It's new and different to the older generations, but they can be taught and do want to learn it. It just takes patience!

Another assumption you should avoid is that your older workers are not receptive to change. Actually they are quite the opposite of this. If you look back to Chapter 2, you'll see the history that both the Radio Babies and Baby Boomers have experienced in their lifetimes—lots and lots of change! They are very willing to change but don't want to make changes for no logical reason. The change needs to produce a result that will have a positive impact on the company, employees, and/or customers. To successfully get them to accept the change, involve them in the solution, communicate with them, and provide them with the appropriate tools and resources to ensure a smooth transition. Definitely do not arbitrarily implement a change without including them or getting their thoughts.

Tip #6: Respect differences in communication styles

The key to any successful relationship rests on communication. We all have different styles and ways we prefer to communicate that are based on many factors, including age. Gen Ys and Gen Xers tend to rely heavily on technology for communication, whether it is e-mail, voice mail, or even instant messenger clients such as AOL's AIM. At the same time, these younger generations are also very comfortable with key communications being shared over an informal, casual atmosphere such as lunch. These methods of communication can be extremely infuriating to the older generations ,who were raised to communicate face to face in the office when you had an issue because it was the right thing to do (and these technological options didn't exist).

As a younger boss, you need to respect this difference and balance your communications with your older direct reports to include more face-to-face conversations, even if it takes more time, and carefully select the right place for communications to ensure everyone is comfortable. It really isn't all about you. The result will be more productive communications all around.

Remember: The older generation was young once, and you will be old someday too. Individuals from different generations working together is an opportunity for everyone to learn. Your best solutions are going to come from learning from older workers' experiences and applying those experiences to your fresh new ideas. It's a give and take—don't forget to give a little too.

Summary

Nobody ever said being the boss—or being the subordinate—was easy! Whether you are a young boss of older workers or vice versa, don't make it harder than it has to be. The key is to learn to understand and respect the differences of the employees you work with or for.

Case Study: Younger Managing Older Workers

Susan, a 27-year-old manager in accounting, has come to you, the HR rep, for advice. Susan manages six staff, all of whom are 10–15 years older than her. Although she has an MBA and is a CPA, along with 10 years' experience in various accounting positions, her direct reports treat her as their daughter rather than their supervisor. Susan dresses and speaks very professionally, and is very knowledgeable about the company and its business imperatives. Older staff constantly remind her of her age with comments such as, "I've got underwear older than you." Susan has been the accounting manager for only eight months, but she is seriously thinking of leaving the company.

Question for Discussion

1. What advice can you give her to help build a team that respects her and her abilities?

Solution

The Baby Boomers who are Susan's direct reports may instinctively treat her as their daughter rather than as their manager. Because they've been in the workplace longer, they likely have some work styles and methods that have become habit. Susan's fresh approach and ideas may be difficult to accept for this reason, especially coming from one "so young."

The situation should be dealt with immediately, because Susan has already thought about leaving. If her concerns aren't addressed, another company will benefit from this company's inaction. The entire accounting department could benefit from well-designed teambuilding workshops that provide an opportunity for them to build mutual respect. But more than that, Susan's manager, or another senior-level, respected employee, could communicate to Susan's direct reports his support for Susan while highlighting her expertise and making it known that they are expected to afford her the respect to which she is entitled.

Chapter 12

They Want *What?!* Working With the Gen Y Entitlement Mindset

"Have you heard about the newest doll? It's a teenager doll. You wind it up, and it resents you for it." —Anonymous

Linda and Robin:

Perhaps you're one of the many 45-and-older workers who cannot relate to what you view as the entitlement mindset of the new workforce—Generation Y. As a manager, you may understand that it is critical to establish a workplace environment that fosters creativity and productive effort. Perhaps you are a member of a task force or project team that has members who are in their early 20s, and you want to encourage their effort and participation. In any event, this question has undoubtedly crossed your mind at least on one occasion: Who are these people, and what do they want?!

During the early years of Generation X, "planned parenting" often meant contraceptives or abortions. For Generation Y, this more likely means visits to the fertility clinic! Consequently, in 1998 the number of children in the United States surpassed the Baby Boomer era peak, and college enrollment is projected to grow by about 300,000 per year over the next few years (Howe and Strauss 2000).

In Chapter 2, we provided some context around how Gen Y grew up and the factors that have influenced their perspectives and approach to the world of work. Now let's get specific about ways to encourage and foster a mindset that is receptive to constructive criticism, understanding that all assignments won't be high-level assignments, and accepting of a salary commensurate with their experience, skills, and abilities.

The Gen Ys we interviewed expressed an interest in collaboration and being a part of a team effort in the workplace. They have grown accustomed to being on teams through their involvement in sports such as soccer. For many Gen Ys, this involvement started well before they were even in first grade. They told us that they believe they need to be serious in the workplace and make positive changes to ensure our country remains competitive and service-driven. Yes, these comments came from people between the ages of 14 and 25!

In this chapter, we will address some of the entitlements the youngest members of the workforce told us they expect, and suggest ways we can either accede to these requests or help Gen Ys understand which expectations are not realistic—and why.

Entitlement to cutting-edge technology

One aspect of work that Gen Ys feel entitled to is cutting-edge technology. They do not want to work for companies that think so little of their employees and customers that they do not invest in equipment and processes that are efficient and easy to use. People we interviewed said that they want technology, not just to indulge them; but so they can work faster and better. As Martha Stewart would say, "That's a good thing."

If your organization does not have the budget to continually invest in the latest technology, we recommend that, at the least, you empower your youngest workers to experiment with the most efficient ways to use the technology you have. They are not afraid to experiment and will likely find a more efficient way to utilize what technology you have to help the company overall.

In the workplace, there are many lessons we can learn about how to more effectively use the resources we have.

Here is a story from one Baby Boomer that isn't too uncommon for any of the older generations (including Gen Xers!):

I was taking a shopping trip with a friend and her 19-year-old daughter recently. I had to make a couple of business calls on my cell phone while en route. One of the people called me back while I was on another call and left a voice message. I expressed frustration when the caller didn't leave his or her callback number because I had closed up my file with phone numbers. My 19-year-old companion said, "Just check their number on your phone book feature." I was woefully ignorant of the fact that I had this feature. She graciously showed me how to access previously called numbers and a few other features I didn't know I had!

Entitlement to a conflict-free workplace

Perhaps Gen Y's parents and family loved and adored them; however, customers and coworkers may not have the same level of patience and understanding. We can't realistically wrap our employees in a cocoon free from anxiety, rudeness, disagreement, or worries of any kind. Even if we could, once they leave the workplace to go out into the rest of the world, they must face controversy and conflict.

Our client companies that have the most success with recruiting and developing Gen Ys have been very up-front and straightforward about the workplace environment during the interview process. If they must work in a customer service capacity, potential employees are told that they will encounter rude, angry, frustrated customers. If they must work with obstinate coworkers, they are told that they will be provided with some conflict resolution education in order to cope. The good news is that the younger employees we interviewed are less willing to accept rude behavior on the part of coworkers and will call them on it, whether they are older or younger. And the younger employees also expressed appreciation for the companies that were open from the get-go about potential conflict that could occur on the job and how the company would support them in obtaining the skills to handle these situations.

We do find that conflict resolution skill-building is essential in today's workplace and is particularly helpful for the newest entrants. Topics such as handling anger (theirs and others'), win-win confrontations, and providing constructive criticism are especially helpful. Gen Ys don't feel they are alone, however, in needing this training. In fact, they feel all workers would benefit from skill-building in conflict resolution because we are becoming such a "service" society. For our businesses to succeed, everyone must learn (or continue) to "positively" deal with conflict and criticism.

Entitlement to constant feedback

We found that Gen Xers want more frequent feedback than once-a-year performance reviews, and Gen Ys want *daily* feedback. They've grown up receiving constant feedback and positive recognition from parents, teachers, coaches, and electronics (games). They told us they feel lost at work if they don't continue to receive this immediate feedback from coworkers and their supervisor, because it either provides reassurance that they are on the right track, or that they need to change courses to successfully meet the ultimate end goal or expectation. Without the feedback, they assume they are not adding value and may seek an opportunity elsewhere where they receive feedback, both positive and constructive.

This does not mean that supervisors must conduct structured, detailed performance reviews every week with Gen Y workers. This does mean, however, that feedback should be built around positive or negative critical incidents and given close to the time the incident occurred. Remember that positive feedback can come in many forms, as simple as a pat on the back, a Post-it note on the desk, an e-mail, or even an IM (instant message). The key is to provide the feedback. That's good advice for any age group!

At the same time, constructive criticism or negative incidents need to be addressed too. We are not saying that anyone younger than 25 is incapable of receiving constructive criticism. But rather, we suggest the feedback should be clear, specific, and concrete. "You can't write reports" will not be helpful. "When you do your monthly report, I need this specific information: a, b, and c. I need this because..." will be helpful. We've found that Gen Ys want and need clear, concrete goals. We've found Gen Ys to be blunt when it comes to expressing their views, and if the "why" is provided when you express your views, we believe that in time this generation will learn to accept opposing ideas in the spirit of growth and development.

Entitlement to a high salary

What is considered a "high salary"? We've seen many situations in which someone in a younger generation is seeking a salary double his or her worth. But at the same time we've also seen companies try to undercut the salary of a younger candidate, only fueling this entitlement mindset.

For example, Linda recently helped a young woman, about 23, revise her resume so she could move on to her next position. The young woman said that she and many of her friends have traveled a great deal across the United States and in other countries. They have had rich experiences that have given them ideas, values, and expertise beyond their years (in their opinion). Because of this she said many people in her age group feel that they should be able to walk into an organization and expect a high salary. And a corner office. And flexible benefits. After all, they have a lot to contribute. Unfortunately, many in this younger generation don't have experience with frequent face-to-face interaction with others, she admitted—something that her travels gave her in spades. Her experiences allowed her to hone her *in-person* social skills while many of her peers were only developing *online* social skills.

Linda and I have both seen a common theme emerging with many companies trying to get these "young pups" as cheap as they can. Unfortunately, the economy was recessed from about 2001 until 2005, which means many individuals were lucky to find jobs. Many companies have taken advantage of the recession and lowered salaries, especially to the younger, entry-level workers.

Although we agree that we don't need to automatically pay Gen Ys a "high salary" with a corner office and dream benefits, we do feel we need to consider their background and experiences. We don't just want a warm body, but rather the cream of the crop—someone with some life experiences and strong communication skills. We may need to pay more for this, but remember: Pay doesn't always come in the form of dollars.

If your organization cannot, or chooses not to, offer high salaries for younger employees, you might consider other enticements that appeal to Gen Ys. For example, Xerox uses the phrase "Express Yourself" in its recruiting campaign for colleges. This puts one of their core values out there—that employees are encouraged and recognized for sharing their ideas and perspectives. We also recommend that you provide education on one-on-one communication and presentation skills to provide employees with the ability to clearly articulate their ideas and perspectives.

Pay *is* important to the Gen Ys! It was the number-one response to our question about what entices them to join an organization. But as older generations are, they are looking at the whole package. What do you offer in the form of benefits that are beneficial to them? What opportunities are there for growth and development (and how soon)? What is the work environment like—casual, fun, flexible?

Once you have Gen Ys on board with you, we believe that if you commit to listening to younger workers' ideas and provide them with intrapreneurship opportunities, they will in turn show commitment to your organization—high salary or no high salary.

Although there are many similarities that help us group individuals by generations, do not be quick to generalize everyone in one generation as the same. Not all Gen Ys are colorfully expressed from hair to clothes to piercings. Not all Gen Ys show up late to work or leave when the clock strikes 4:59. Not all Gen Ys have an entitlement mindset to salary.

Truly, you need to find what motivates each of them and feed that motivation.

Robin:

I have had a Gen Y work for me for more than two years. She is by far the best employee I have ever had. She is extremely reliable, more than punctual, and never once has been lined up at the door ready to leave at the end of the day.

Though I wouldn't say money isn't important, it definitely isn't the focus for this Gen Y. I am confident she isn't alone (because I've seen her friends' commitment to work). If you shed the stereotype glasses, you might find some stellar employees and diminish some of the entitlement mindset that we too are feeding.

Summary

Linda and Robin:

It is not a myth that many individuals in Generation Y have an entitlement mindset; however, it is a myth that this mindset cannot be overcome. Your best solution will be to listen to the Gen Ys that work for you, and provide the tools and resources to help them succeed, from technology to training to growth opportunity. Providing regular and constant feedback while listening to and respecting their ideas will go a long way in both enticing and retaining this generation.

Case Study: Entitlement Mentality

Ruth, the VP of finance, is frustrated. One of her best employees, Bill, is being stubborn on a matter that deeply concerns Ruth. Bill is a 26-year-old newly appointed accounting manager. Bill has an MBA, is a CPA, and just started with the organization 18 months ago as assistant accounting manager. Ruth thinks his appointment to manager about a month ago indicates a rapid rise within the company. Ruth was with the organization for 12 years before she was appointed to her current position, and she put in many weekends and late evenings along the way. Bill met with Ruth yesterday on a topic he has raised three previous times: flexible hours and telecommuting. Although the company hours are 8 a.m.–5 p.m. Monday through Friday, Bill wants to work 10 a.m.–7 p.m. two days a week and work from home three days a week. No other employee in the 200-employee company has ever insisted on a schedule such as this. Bill insists that, if this can't be worked out, he'll accept another offer he has received from a competitor company. He has told Ruth he wants an answer today.

Questions for Discussion

1. Do you believe Bill is being unreasonable in his request? Why or why not?

2. Do you think some embedded personal beliefs are getting in the way of resolving this problem? If so, what might they be?

3. What options would you suggest to come to a win-win solution?

Solution

Bill certainly believes that his request is reasonable. He is negotiating different hours and the ability to work at home, not permission to work with less commitment or zeal. He is concentrating on results, not the process through which results are obtained. Bill is not interested in what other employees have or have not done before him; his focus is on his needs and how they can be met. This may be different from Ruth's approach; that doesn't make it wrong.

Ruth's embedded belief seems to be that you follow the company's "rules" whether you like them or not. She had to, so why shouldn't younger employees do the same? She had to work weekends and "pay her dues"—isn't this just the way things are in business?

Bill is just as firmly entrenched in his belief that organizations should flex to the needs of their productive employees. Unless Ruth can provide him with sound business reasons why his requests can't be met, he believes that Ruth is simply being stubborn. He believes he's entitled to a response favorable to his request—now.

There are options for a win–win solution, as there are in many situations of this nature. Ruth should consider what she *needs*, not what she *wants*. She needs an accounting manager who is competent and productive. She needs to have management staff stay with the organization for a long enough period of time to contribute and provide value. Ruth can explore whether Bill's position, or others within the finance division, are amenable to telecommuting. Perhaps Bill could telecommute two or three days a week and be on site during key meetings and conferences. Technology could bring him into the organization in "real time" when he's in his home office.

Exploring these options may take some time, so Ruth could ask for Bill's assistance in collecting information on technology options. Bill would be engaged in the process of exploration and receive his response as quickly as he can collect information and ideas.

Ruth should, in the meantime, set firm expectations for the level of work that will be required from anyone who telecommutes. If the work falls behind qualitatively or quantitatively, an employee's flexibility on telecommuting could be curtailed.

To prevent this scenario from repeating itself, the organization can be more explicit about promotional opportunities and job flexibility in the interview and on-boarding process. This is the time to establish concrete, realistic expectations around career progression and flexibility for hours.

Chapter 13

Tailoring Training and Development Across Generations

Linda and Robin:

Throughout this book, we've asserted that one size does not fit all when it comes to recruiting and retaining different age groups. Training and development, a huge investment in time and money in many organizations, can be most effective when the design and implementation takes generational differences into account. In this chapter, we'll address how astute trainers develop and deliver training efforts in a way that capitalizes on the skills and contributions of each participant, regardless of age.

In our research, we've observed a common trend with all the generations: a desire to grow and develop professionally and personally. Each of the generations had a different focus in terms of what they wanted in order to grow and learn. The way individuals learn varies by generation (see Table 13-1). Organizations that understand how to tailor training and development to incorporate the unique needs of different age groups will find their investment leveraged to the fullest extent.

Effective training for Radio Babies

As we pointed out, Radio Babies spent their early years in the world of work during a time when there were no VCRs or DVDs. Training, when it was conducted, was typically on-the-job training and was directed specifically at doing the job at hand. Growing organizations did not have the luxury of pulling employees away from "the line" for extended periods of time to sit in a classroom on-site, much less afford to send them to conference centers and universities. Because of this background, many Radio Babies grew accustomed to straightforward lecture-style training. Some of the Radio Babies we interviewed said that *any* opportunity to sit in a classroom was special because their education was limited to some high school or at most a high school diploma.

If any age group will turn up early for training, it will be the Radio Babies. They want to get a good seat so that they can hear and see clearly (or sit with their friends).

They want to look over the workbook or training materials to get a level of comfort with what's going to be covered. We recommend that you have your coffee and continental breakfast out early for these folks...at least a half hour prior to the start of the workshop.

For Radio Babies, respect for authority figures is high. The teacher, or trainer, is a person they respect at the very least for the fact that they're a teacher. This in part explains why Radio Babies are more likely to tolerate long periods of training in which a lecture style is used. Radio Babies didn't grow up with technology, or the expectation that others would entertain them as they learned. Rather, their expectation is that they will listen and the teacher will impart knowledge.

Radio Baby participants in the training we've conducted over the years are very appreciative of the use of real-world case studies during training. This provides them with an opportunity to shine in breakout groups because they can share their years of experience in responding to discussion questions. One of their pet peeves we uncovered during the interviews is that younger workshop participants want to talk, talk, and talk some more when "they don't know what they're talking about." Radio Babies will listen to others in a group setting, however, if they are afforded respect when it's their turn to add to the discussion. They also appreciate being personally acknowledged for insights and ideas by the trainer.

Radio Babies indicated during our research that they highly value working for secure, profitable organizations. When they have an opportunity to attend training that will help them—and other employees—support the company's "bottom line" they're receptive to taking the time to learn. Even when Radio Babies cannot appreciate the connection between a training event and success in their department, division, or company, they'll still attend out of respect for their gainful employment. They will not, however, be as motivated to stay engaged in the process as when they fully "get" the reason the training is being conducted. To us, it makes good business sense to align all training activities with the strategic objectives of the organization! Additionally, when this fact is communicated to workshop participants of any age, there will be more buy-in to attend and participate fully.

Trainers may have to do some follow-up evaluations after the day of training to elicit Radio Babies' true feelings about the value of training. Because of their respect for trainers, they may be too nice on the "day of" evaluation instrument and not write remarks that seem negative. Radio Babies may be concerned that the evaluations are going to "the top" and would reflect poorly on a trainer trying to do a good job.

We recommend that, if you're responsible for training, you develop a longer-term evaluation plan that circles back with participants for one-on-one input. You could also conduct small focus groups a month or two following training events to discover how participants have used training techniques, and brainstorm additional ways to use acquired knowledge.

Many of the Radio Babies we spoke with said they're at a point in their career at which they still want to learn job-related skills; however, they're just as interested in learning peripheral skills that are fun and challenging. Some of the younger Radio Babies are far from ready to hang up their accumulated skills and experiences, and still want to contribute to the world of work and volunteer activities. If your organization needs team facilitators, for example, consider training older employees who would appreciate learning new skills and using them outside their immediate job responsibilities.

Effective training for Baby Boomers

Baby Boomers had to share space when they were growing up. They had to share space at school, in extracurricular activities, and at home...because there are so many of them! Boomers became accustomed to being with others and sharing activities in a team setting, and this transfers to the training environment. Boomers are usually quite comfortable engaging in learning activities that mean working as part of a group and can get annoyed when group members don't "play nice." (Playing nice often translates to sharing ideas, resources, and speaking time.)

The Boomers we interviewed said they enjoy and appreciate some social time before training begins so they can have an opportunity to meet people they'll be spending time with over the next few hours or days. So we encourage you to greet Boomers as they enter the training room, show them where to get coffee, and introduce them to another participant or two. If you intersperse activities throughout the workshop that break people into different groups, Boomers will enjoy getting to know people other than those sitting at the table with them when they first arrived.

Many Boomers have had the opportunity throughout their career to serve in various capacities on teams—from team leader to team facilitator to individual contributor. Often, they're comfortable in a training environment going from role to role and enjoy the variety. Depending on their personality, of course, some may appreciate leadership roles more than others. The idea is to provide activities that give Boomers a chance to talk and engage with others in the workshop so they get an opportunity for input and recognition from their peers.

The Boomers we interviewed like to understand how the training they participate in supports the organization's business imperatives and strategic objectives. Many grew up in an era when training gurus such as Tom Peters and Stephen Covey were espousing long-term planning and leadership, so they want to be impressed with the training's "big picture" effect. In the overview portion of training, Boomers really appreciate hearing objectives that are aligned with their division's or the organization's objectives and goals. Then they have an idea of the ways in which what they're about to learn supports team efforts.

Boomers definitely like to share their perspectives during training, as well as input afterwards as to how the training went. They'll appreciate an opportunity to evaluate the training immediately following the session, and in focus groups or within their department later. Boomers, we've found, are especially mindful of the way training impacts the effort of their immediate department or division, and will provide feedback with that focus.

The youngest Boomers were born in 1964 and are still projecting several work years ahead. Their primary interests revolve around acquiring the skills and competencies they need to compete with a younger workforce. Many Boomers we interviewed were less interested in the latest technology for its own sake than for the knowledge that it will keep them "on top of the heap." Boomers are starting to look around them and see younger, fresher faces vying for their positions. They want to stay sharp to stay ahead, so they're excited about training that provides state-of-the-art skills and leadership techniques.

Effective training for Gen Xers

The Gen Xers we interviewed had one common message to trainers: Give us activities and case studies that are on point. Do *not* waste time with "feel-good" activities that don't relate exactly to what the training is all about. One interviewee said, "The facilitator of one workshop made us write with our left hand if we were right-handed so we'd feel what it's like to 'get outside your comfort zone.' How stupid."

Gen Xers also told us they enjoy the opportunity to work on individual exercises, and then report out on their own, as opposed to being part of a team. Remember that these are people who've grown up as "latchkey" children, in one-child families, and schlepping back and forth to a different parent's home every other weekend. Many don't feel an overwhelming need to be involved in team activities. Just tell them what you want done, give them the resources, and step back. They don't need praise from the trainer for their input; they're fine with the satisfaction of doing an activity well.

A major complaint from the Gen Xers we interviewed is that too many trainers provide case studies and discussion questions and then expect "only one answer." These Xers were very annoyed that multiple perspectives weren't solicited and respected. In other words, the "teacher" isn't afforded the right to have the final answer to questions or issues under discussion. Trainers should expect to be challenged during the course of the training event, especially if they are bold enough to say something such as, "This is the only way to address this issue."

We've learned that it's very important to balance "listening" with "telling" to engage Gen Xers. The Gen Xers we interviewed said they appreciate trainers who:

❑ Maintain eye contact with *all* workshop participants during training.

❑ Ask follow-up questions to participants' comments and inquiries.

❑ Don't interrupt participants who are sharing an idea or perspective.

❑ Paraphrase to ensure understanding before jotting participants' comments on a flip chart or white board.

Students of any age won't experience anything but drowsiness if trainers aren't astute enough to balance "telling" and "listening."

Gen Xers, we found, are keenly interested in working with an organization with a mission they can support on a personal level. Training is no exception—they want to understand how any training they take the time to attend will help them support the company's mission. In the PR pieces for training, it's important to explain the training objectives, what trainees will be able to do as a result of the training, and how specifically the training ties in with the organization's vision and mission. Otherwise, you won't even get Gen Xers to attend (voluntary) training, much less stay in a training session for any length of time.

Gen Xers don't respect trainers simply because they are in the front of the room. They respect knowledge and the ability to succinctly transfer that knowledge. If they're not receiving what they want and need, the Xers we interviewed acknowledged that they would speak up and out during the training. They will let the trainer know, often in front of the entire workshop, when they don't believe the information is valuable or correct. In other words, if you're training Xers you definitely want to make sure you've done your homework and are very knowledgeable about the subject matter you're covering.

Gen Xers are amenable to learning tailored techniques and skills that will help them in their current position, but they also are keenly interested in acquiring transferable skills and knowledge to take on to their next job. Trainers who can generalize how techniques and skills will work in many environments will capture Xers' attention much more readily.

We have one final suggestion. Steadfastly follow the rule of "start on time/end on time" with Gen Xers. Many will have come to the training from dropping off their children at daycare or picking up the dry cleaning. They may need to leave right at the end time in order to retrieve the children from daycare so they don't have to pay for an extra 20 minutes (it's expensive!). Their time is precious to them and they expect trainers to use it wisely.

Effective training for Gen Ys

The key point to remember in designing training for Gen Y participants is that you'll need to capture and keep their attention. This is a generation that is accustomed to multi-tasking and may be text-messaging friends during training that is interesting, let alone training that they deem boring. This is definitely the age group for whom trainers will want to provide technology and use a variety of teaching methods. If you're of the opinion that training does not have to be entertaining, you're not likely to be successful with Gen Ys. Music used as background and to emphasize key points is effective. Games that engage them individually and in teams are musts during training. If you can establish interactive computer simulations, that's perfect.

Trainers who are most effective with Gen Ys are those who are casual and laid-back in their training style. A conversational and friendly tone is much more accepted than the lecture method. If the trainer can introduce real scenarios that occur frequently and they can relate to, there will be much for discussion and participation. We encourage you to bring focus groups together during the design phase of training to tap into their issues and perspectives.

We found that many Gen Ys don't see the big fuss about arriving early for training, let alone "right on the dot." They enjoy a more flexible time frame for the start of training activities. Many told us that they've observed that the first 10 minutes are "boring, housekeeping kinds of things" they don't need to hear. If you want to get Gen Ys in the door early, announce a giveaway or activity that's fun...which will occur in the first five minutes.

Gen Ys are image-conscious for themselves, their friends, and the organization for which they work. If you can relate training to the company's core values and brand, you'll have a much better chance of capturing their interest. Saying, "You have to learn this because I said so" is much less effective than saying, "Our brand is *Inspired Science...Trusted Solutions* (Meridian Bioscience, Cincinnati, Ohio) and this training will demonstrate how you can live that in your work on a daily basis."

Gen Ys are most likely to need frequent recognition and feedback for their participation. Trainers who ask questions, receive responses, and comment positively on those responses will enjoy more interactive sessions. We don't recommend that you offer insincere praise, however. Remember that Gen Ys possess B.S. radar just as the Xers before them!

If you want to take some steps in advance of workshops to encourage participation by Gen Ys, consider asking two or three people to be prepared to share their perspective on some of the discussion questions you plan to use. For that matter, why not share your workbook ahead of time for people to review? If there are articles or books you intend to use as a reference, provide an advance reading list.

A fun workshop environment is essential for keeping the interest and energy level high with Gen Ys. Quiz-game competitions (Jeopardy, for example) are fun. Prizes for individual and group projects are fun. Trainers who are casual and tell an occasional appropriate joke are fun. Lectures, straight PowerPoint presentations, written quizzes, and workshops with no toys to play with are *not* fun.

Don't be afraid to include activities that help yourself as the trainer and the participants to gain focus and concentration. Demonstrate a few Pilates or t'ai chi moves and take stretch breaks from time to time to let people unwind. Place bowls of peppermints on the tables—this candy enhances energy and improves the air quality!

Summary

Effective trainers are accustomed to designing workshops that include a variety of teaching methods and approaches. This mindset well serves trainers who are faced with training events with participants of all age groups in attendance. The underlying principle, as in our other chapters, is to treat trainees of all ages with respect for what they can contribute. Another fundamental for success is to design opportunities for interaction among participants and fun activities that make the trainees forget they're "in school." A wonderful resource for training design is the Website for The American Society for Training and Development (*www.astd.org*).

Table 13-1: Training different generations

Radio Babies	Baby Boomers	Gen-Xers	Gen-Ys
Lecture style is acceptable.	Include team activities in teaching methods.	Include lots of activities and individual report-outs.	Use technology and lots of variety in teaching methods.
Respect their experience and opinion in case studies.	Let participants experience different team roles (such as leader).	"One solution" to case studies is unacceptable.	"One solution" to case studies is unacceptable; want casual . discussion.
Align training with company's bottom-line success.	Align training with company's strategic plan.	Align training with company's mission.	Align training with company's values and positive image.
Will be respectful in evaluation comments at end of session.	Will want to evaluate at end of session and at follow-up times.	Will provide feedback during the session and won't patronize trainer.	Will provide feedback during the session and expect praise for it.
Interested in adding skills just for fun.	Want deliverables that ensure job survival.	Want skills that are transferable to other companies.	Want fun skills that are transferable to other companies.

Will arrive at workshop early.	Will want social time during workshop.	Start on time/end on time expectation.	Start on time but I may be late/end early expectation.
Want trainer to acknowledge their input.	Want other participants to acknowledge their input.	Don't need anyone's acknowledgment.	Want trainer to *frequently* acknowledge their input.

Case Study: Training for the Generations

Bill rushed into the training room 10 minutes before the scheduled start time. He had hoped to arrive early enough to test the AV equipment and place handouts on the tables before participants started coming in. He looked around as he walked toward the front of the room, and he could tell that about half of the registrants were already there, sitting in an awkward silence. Typically, Bill liked to greet people before he began his workshops, but today he'd just have to forego that nicety and make sure he was set up properly. He was an external consultant coming into the organization's training room, so he was hopeful that everyone knew where coffee was located and was acquainted with at least one or two other coworkers at the training.

Bill hurriedly set up his laptop and projector, focusing on what he was doing instead of people coming in and out of the room. At five minutes after scheduled start time, he was ready to go. He mentally shifted into "show time" mode and looked up to greet the class with a smile.

Bill was dismayed at what he saw as he looked out over the room. The coffee and continental breakfast that was supposed to be set up in the back of the room wasn't there. There were four tables set up in rounds to seat eight, instead of six tables set up to seat six. All the older participants were huddled around two of the tables...one for men and one for women. Supervisors had been asked to provide participants with their workbook materials the previous day, yet only about a third of the trainees had a workbook in front of them. Bill mentally gulped, but cheerfully welcomed everyone and told his favorite joke that always loosened people up. No one laughed.

Bill ignored the lack of response and jumped right into his slide presentation, with the first slide showing the workshop objectives. He had been told that these objectives were going to be shared with participants in the training publicity, so he only spent a moment reviewing them before moving on to logistics such as breaks and lunch arrangements. He thought this would settle people in to concentrate on the topic at hand, but he sensed a restlessness across the room.

Bill moved on to a breakout activity with a case study—he had to get those two tables huddled together mixed up! When he asked people to "count off" for the breakout groups, they seemed reluctant to leave the table where they were sitting. Bill just joked about shaking things up as people slowly moved into discussion groups.

There was a tenseness in the air for the first 90 minutes, and by the time he was ready to call the first break, Bill didn't know who was more uncomfortable—him or the workshop participants. This was not going as planned, and he had to come up with something during the 15-minute break to turn things around.

Questions for Discussion

1. What could Bill have done differently to set a positive tone at the beginning of the workshop that would appeal to participants of all ages?
2. Do you have any suggestions for how Bill can salvage the day?

Solution

There's no question that it's important to be prepared with room set-up, AV equipment, and handouts prior to the start of the workshop. This preparation enhances a trainer's credibility. If Bill wanted to be ready at the appointed start time, he could have arranged his schedule so that he would arrive at least 30 minutes early. If traffic or some other delay was going to result in his running behind, he could have contacted a pre-determined person at the organization to help him put handouts on tables (dropped off in advance of the training day) or ensure the room was set up appropriately. Greeting people as they enter training is a way to make them feel welcome, and this is especially important for Boomers and Gen Ys. Having coffee or juice for a morning workshop is critical! Even if he had to cut a portion short later in the day, Bill would have provided a more welcoming environment if he made sure that participants were greeted, had coffee, were directed to a table, and had an opportunity to meet other students.

Bill had an opportunity to get the "pulse" of the room early on, when people didn't respond to humor that normally was effective. For later reflection, this may be a clue that his jokes and stories are dated and no longer funny. He missed the chance to align objectives by not checking to see if the stated objectives were in tune with the participants' expectations. For different reasons, this is important for each and every participant. He framed the workshop as being structured and rigid by staying on task the moment he walked into the room, head down and "on a mission." He lost the younger participants at that moment.

Bill has a very short time to decide how to capture peoples' attention and interest. He should take participants back to the beginning of the workshop and revisit the objectives. Bill should be candid and admit that he was not effective in drawing them in and setting a positive, interactive tone at the beginning. (It's likely that a couple of Gen X participants told him this during the break!) He can ask for their forgiveness and help in "regrouping." If a trainer is sincere, people will generally give him or her a second chance. He could start with the objectives and ask them to add their expectations and issues around the topic, writing them down and gaining clarification as people talk. He may need to throw out some of his agenda items and focus on two or three areas that are of most concern to participants. He may need to lead a discussion of real time issues rather than use prepared scenarios. Most importantly, he needs to let people know that he's willing to be flexible in order to cover areas that will be most helpful to them.

Chapter 14

Building a Bridge
Across the Generations

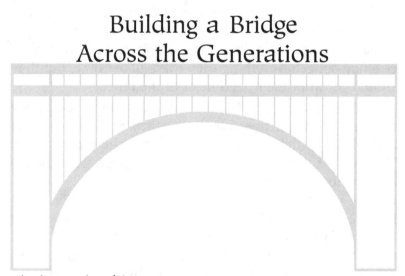

Linda and Robin:

So...what are we to make of all this? What are the keys to help us recruit, develop, and retain quality staff in each age group? We have some suggestions.

Key #1: One size does not fit all:
Tailor your message

Across the generations a pattern emerged during our interviews: All age groups want respect. All age groups desire flexibility in work arrangements. However, this desire for respect and flexibility manifests itself in different ways from generation to generation.

We are not suggesting that each and every individual in a 5,000-employee company should have every single work arrangement or benefit he or she desires. We *are* recommending that leaders periodically "check in" with employees to determine the workplace attributes that are most desirable. Budgeted dollars can then be channeled into areas that will result in the most mileage in terms of job satisfaction and organizational commitment. All employees may not get everything they *want* all the time, but they should get what they *need* most of the time.

The best way to do this is to ask your employees. They can tell you what they have that they really appreciate and what else they need or would simply be nice to have. You may be surprised at some of their suggestions. Many may be low-cost—or even no cost—and actually accommodate individuals in more than one generation. Plus, you may be able to offer some sort of cafeteria plan that allows the employees to select the benefits they need (such as childcare versus aging parent care). The key to all of these solutions will rest on how much and how well you communicate what you offer and why, as well as what you can't offer (now) and why.

The "one size doesn't fit all" mindset also applies to how you train and develop your staff. We saw a common trend with all the generations of a desire to grow and develop, but each of the generations had a different focus for what and how they wanted to grow, develop, and learn. Organizations need to be aware of these different needs or reasons in order to learn and address them individually, rather than trying to make training and development fit everyone. Plus, the way an individual learns varies by generation (see Table 13-1), and the organization that accommodates these different learning styles will see a huge benefit in the return on investment for training and even in the retention of the staff being trained.

Key #2: Leverage the skills and competencies available in all age groups

In today's competitive, global marketplace, each generation's skillset is crucial to gain competitive advantage.

Linda:

My technology mentor is my co-author, Robin. She's 18 years younger than I am, and I couldn't care less. She possesses expertise in computer technology that I do not. On the other hand, some of my colleagues are 10–15 years older than me. So I also value and depend on the wisdom that comes from having "been there, done that."

Robin:

Likewise, my true mentor is Linda! She actually was one of my professors during my graduate studies. She encouraged me and provided me with the tools to begin my human resources consulting practice more than 10 years ago. Throughout my consulting career, she's been a wonderful resource of knowledge for me. I love to try new and different angles on things, but I don't want to reinvent the wheel. Linda's "been there, done that" and has shed light on many situations I've faced.

Linda and Robin:

As with most of our recommendations, if you ask employees for ideas on how to capitalize on everyone's different or unique contributions, you will find a number of wonderful and easy-to-implement solutions. As a group, brainstorm those contributions and develop ways to capitalize on them. As we have personally found, you will find that employees have a great deal to offer one another. Remember the commercial in which the young guy goes into the "big" boss's office for coaching: Once the door is shut, the young guy helps the boss with stock trades on the computer and the boss helps the younger guy with life skills. Real life can be that way!

In a marketplace that is now and will remain highly competitive, each employee's contributions must be leveraged if we want our organizations to survive and thrive.

Key #3: Build a brand as an organization that values diversity.

Perhaps you're thinking, "Whoa...when did this become a marketing book?!" The truth is, our marketing colleagues have some excellent points about building a brand that can be adapted for HR and OD (organizational development) professionals.

Let's define "branding" first. A brand can be:
- ❏ The essence of who you are.
- ❏ Features and attributes.

❑ Performance.

❑ A set of values.

There are several proactive ways to build a brand as a company that values all age groups:

Drive out fear. Ensure that employees understand that skills, knowledge, and abilities matter. Age is just a number. Decisions about people aren't made based on their age. If your employees are more concerned about coloring their gray hair to stay young-looking than helping your company succeed, you're not leveraging everyone's talents to the fullest. You need to be sure you have a system in place to recognize and reward the performance of all your employees, regardless of age or tenure with the organization.

Establish process checkpoints and measures. No, we are not leading you down the Affirmative Action path. We are suggesting that you establish success criteria such as retention of quality staff from all age groups (diversify your teams and departments); reduction in employee and management time diverted to conflict and negative infighting because they don't understand each other (train staff on the value of differences and address those gaps and problems head-on); and increased productivity—qualitatively and quantitatively—in work groups that are diverse in terms of age (develop ways to capitalize on the differences through mentoring or cross-training). Check the results periodically—a few times a year.

Align values across the organization. Perhaps the company's leadership has decided that a core value is "embracing diversity." The leadership team may be clear among themselves how that value looks in action, but their understanding needs to be shared and communicated effectively across all levels of the organization. Most importantly, the leadership team will need to demonstrate their commitment to and support of the value through their actions. Core values are just wallpaper when they're simply printed and hung in the lobby. If core values are internalized, no gaps exist in how people think, who they are, and what they do.

Linda:

I joined an organization several years ago in part because a published core value was "embracing diversity." In a management meeting early in my tenure at this company, my peers started telling jokes after the official meeting ended. The kidding around evolved into telling ageist jokes, each one crueler than the next. Even though I was only in my 20s at the time, I thought, "I wouldn't want to work here when I'm 40!" And I didn't. I started my own company instead.

Linda and Robin:

An organization doesn't need to be run with someone walking around policing what folks are saying and doing. However, jokes, comments, or serious statements that are offensive and discriminatory to a generation will result in a tremendous amount of morale problems, not to mention putting the company in legal jeopardy. You will need to be sure you educate your employees on the value of everyone's differences and the unacceptability of these types of "off the cuff" remarks.

In order to build a brand as an organization that appreciates the skills and talents of employees in every age group, take these five important steps:

Determine the key elements of your culture that you can employ to build your brand. Perhaps you'll select the way your organization recruits, promotes, and develops employees as key elements. Explore processes and systems in place. Let's take recruiting as an example. Are your ads written to appeal to different age groups? Do you advertise in sections of the paper read by Generation X and Generation Y? Do you consider applicants older than 50 as viable candidates? If the answer is no to these questions, you have some work to do to expand your recruiting horizons.

Determine the ideal state. What does success look like? What measures are critical to show that your organization has arrived at that ideal state (the brand you want)?

Determine how your employees perceive the culture. At this point it's a good idea to assess whether current employees perceive the organization to have the attributes that represent the brand you're seeking. Several tools and options are available to determine employee perceptions: culture audits, focus groups, and individual interviews, to name a few.

Conduct a gap analysis. Most likely, there will be a gap between the ideal state and actual employee perceptions. Perhaps employees will notice that older workers are hired into the company but not promoted. Perhaps younger employees will perceive that no one listens to their opinions. You can't move forward in the branding process until you're aware of the depth of the chasm between vision and reality.

Take intentional steps to close the gap. The real work is here. Efforts must be made to leverage all employees' skills, knowledge, and abilities to ensure organizational and individual success. The steps required depend on the results of your gap analysis.

The generations are already working to build bridges between themselves. They are learning to take advantage of the desires, needs, and demands of other generations to benefit themselves while trying to share the strengths and skillsets they can offer to make their businesses succeed. It's time for employers to support the building of this generational bridge to retain the brightest and best in their workplace. We have endeavored to provide ideas for action steps throughout this book. Now it's up to you to select the appropriate activities to take advantage of those suggestions!

Summary

We've discovered three keys to building bridges across generations. They're common sense, but not always common practice:

1. Tailor your recruiting message to appeal to the interests and needs of each generation.

2. Understand and draw upon each generation's unique perspectives and experiences.

3. Position your organization as one that values and embraces diversity.

These three keys will open doors to essential dialogue and understanding.

Case Study: Creating a Cohesive Team

As the HR director for Widgets 'R' Us, you've been called upon by the VP of sales and marketing to help them build a more cohesive sales team. He asked for help because the sales force, men and women of all ages, can't seem to pull together and meet sales quotas. You attended a monthly sales meeting this morning, just to observe, and you noticed that the sales manager, a 45-year-old man who's been in his position for 15 years, energetically tried to rally the sales force with phrases such as, "it's all for one and one for all." The younger salesmen and saleswomen sat together in the back of the room, rolling their eyes and pretending to gag. During the lunch break, the sales force clearly sat with people in their own age groups. The tenured sales force bitterly complained at their tables about the "zero work ethic" of "the kids."

Question for Discussion

1. Do you have any ideas for bringing the sales force into a cohesive team?

Solution

This scenario takes place in a manufacturing organization, and manufacturing companies have a unique culture that is far different from that of service or nonprofit companies: Even though women have been moving into the manufacturing workforce over the past two decades, there are still many manufacturing companies that are slow to place (and accept) women in nontraditional female jobs. In the sales department, young men *and* women are trying to make inroads to this culture, and this may be causing some resentment among older male employees.

The VP of sales and marketing identified their problem: a sales team that isn't cohesive and that can't pull together to meet sales quotas. The VP of sales and the sales manager may be Baby Boomers who have spent their lives working, competing with, and pulling together with other Baby Boomers, whereas the younger sales staff may be similar to many Gen Xers who don't necessarily want to work with a team. Their preference may be to have objectives laid out, resources made available, and then turned loose to do their job. A mentor for newer sales reps, available to teach them the organizational culture, provide them with sales techniques, and be there as a sounding board, might be more productive for them than regular, mandatory sales meetings.

The older sales reps are complaining about the "zero work ethic" of "the kids." Coaching for them may prove helpful to provide them with the interaction skills to work with people of younger generations. When young people hear older employees making constant comments about their youth, it may cause them to feel demeaned and disrespected. An important question is this: Are the younger sales reps actually doing less *required* work, thus causing more seasoned vets additional work? The younger employees could also use some coaching on interacting with older workers, who also should be afforded respect for their experience and expertise.

The sales manager may especially require some coaching. He's 45 and has been in his position for 15 years. He has solid experience, to be sure, but he may also need to have some of his "tried and true" ideas challenged.

Chapter 15

Generational Imposters: A Presentation

Linda:

At a recent conference, Robin and I were invited to speak on the topic of recruiting and retaining the four different generations in today's workplace, based on the research of this book. Conference attendees spanned all four generations, but the average age was early 40s.

We decided to do something a little different for our presentation. Robin, in her 30s, dressed as many of us in this country stereotypically think of a woman in her late 50s. She donned a white wig, half glasses, tweed blazer and gray turtleneck, pearls, and sensible shoes. I decided to dress as the stereotypical 20-something (and I'm in my early 50s): jeans, flip-flops, pink-streaked hair, cropped top, and denim jacket.

Robin:

What Linda didn't mention to you was how hard it was for us to come up with our outfits. She is a Baby Boomer who set out to dress as a "younger generation." To really show a difference, she had to go to the extreme stereotype of a Gen Y. On the other hand, as a Gen Xer, I attempted to mimic the "older generations," but everything I picked out was nearly something I would wear. As my 39-year-old husband said, "It's because we are nearly 50 and many of our friends already are." So I attempted to become the Radio Baby imposter that Linda described with multiple pairs of glasses that I constantly misplaced, and bright red lipstick.

Linda:

Although our presentation wasn't until after lunch, we decided to arrive at the conference location a couple of hours early. We began by going over our presentation in a corner of the hotel lobby, near where conference attendees were having lunch. People walking by glanced at Robin without taking much notice. After all, she was dressed "properly" for a business conference. When eyes rested on me, however, it was clear that my appearance was not acceptable!

Robin:

Neither of us was really acceptable, nor comfortable.

Believe it or not, I actually made Linda stomp on her shirt in the hotel room to make it look a little less "pressed." But you do have to picture her in this get-up, relaxed on a couch in the hotel lobby with an iPod in one ear, chomping on a wad of gum, with our presentation slides sprawled out all over the place.

On the other hand, I was feeling very overdressed and extremely hot wearing a turtleneck and a wool jacket. Comfort was definitely not an option as I tried to play my part sitting cross-legged and proper with my notes perfectly stacked on my lap when I'd rather be relaxed, listening to music, and tuning out the world.

Linda:

Part of the reason passersby did a double-take was surely because of my youthful attire as a (clearly) 40-plus woman. The looks sent this message: "Why are you at a business conference dressed the way we would dress to clean our house or paint our garage?" This was a new—and uncomfortable—feeling for me, a Baby Boomer who is always well coifed, perfectly groomed, and in a matching outfit just to go to my mailbox!

Robin:

You would have been amazed at the looks we got—*both* of us. We were facing each other so we could see them coming and going. And we were not actually preparing for our presentation, but putting on a show. Folks didn't know if we were real or dressed up for Halloween. When they'd walk by they'd stare, point, whisper, and even come back a second time to see if they saw what they thought they saw. It was fun.

Linda:

We arrived in the room where we were to speak about 30 minutes early, as participants were coming back and settling in from lunch. We elected to sit in the back of the room for a few minutes to wait for our hostess to finish a conversation so we could greet her and start setting up for our presentation. As I went to retrieve an empty chair, I found that I was the recipient of cold stares. One fellow, who looked to be in his 40s, said incredulously, "Are you here to observe our conference?" I just nodded, smiled, and said that I was observing at the moment. Robin, in the meantime, found an empty chair with no comments from anyone.

The person who invited us to speak had taken us to dinner the previous evening, so she knew us (and what we planned to do for our presentation). She finished her conversation, came back to Robin and me, and greeted each of us warmly with a hug and a hello. I overheard one lady say, "Is *she* a speaker?!" I'm pretty sure the lady wasn't referring to Robin.

Robin and I went to the front of the room and began our prep, setting up the laptop, putting handouts on the tables, and preparing a couple of flip charts. As we passed out handouts, I observed that Robin was met with smiles and hellos. I was met with a few smiles, but more stares at the pink streaks in my hair and my flip-flops.

Robin:

Now, those of you who know Linda and have seen her speak at any event know that what she is describing is extremely unusual for her. Whenever we co-present, she is swarmed the minute she walks in the room with individuals wanting to meet her and ask her questions even before the presentation. While we set up, I got lots of smiles (I thought it was the wig) but did get questions about what we were presenting and how interesting it was going to be. If anyone needed anything, they asked me. I've presented with Linda before so this was a different experience for me; she usually gets this attention.

Linda:

It came time to be introduced. I was introduced first, beginning with "Dr. Linda Gravett is a nationally known speaker and author...." There was an audible gasp from some people in the room—how could someone who looked the way I did be a "nationally known speaker"?!

Robin:

Linda didn't mention that I also had to play Vanna White and show everyone who "Doctor" Gravett was because they all assumed it was me. This was when I noticed the biggest gasp or bit of confusion—"She's the doctor and nationally known speaker? I thought the other gal was...."

Linda:

The responses to Robin and me continued to be different as we went through our program. We did, of course, let participants know right away that we were each dressed as the "stereotypical notion" of a Radio Baby and a Generation Y, respectively. As we presented the research and shared excerpts from our book, people directed most of their questions to Robin—that is, until we started metamorphosing into our real selves. As the program started winding down, Robin took off the white wig and shook out her shoulder-length blond hair. She took off the bifocals and the tweed blazer and turtleneck, revealing a trendy knit top you'd expect to see a person in her 30s wearing. I took the pink streaks out of my hair (they were affixed with bobby pins), exchanged the flip-flops for low heels, and put on a wool blazer instead of the denim jacket. One lady sang out, "She's changing into one of us!" Towards the end of our program, more people started directing questions my way.

Robin:

Now, the true gasp came when folks realized how old I really was. Underneath the getup that I had on, you couldn't tell just how old I might be. So when I pulled off the wig, jacket, and turtleneck and they saw I was a "young" woman in a black dress with a silver belt, everyone's jaw dropped at least two inches. It was fun! Truly, what I was wearing—black top, long black skirt, black boots, and a silver chain belt—could have quickly been met with a black suit jacket and I would have looked as professional as needed for a conference presentation, or so any other Gen Xer might say.

Linda:

Here's one final interesting piece. At the end of a presentation, people typically come up to speakers and ask questions or make comments. The participants that came up to me were in their 20s. The people who came up to Robin were in their 40s and 50s. Typically when we co-present, it's the other way around. Yet we both wrote the book as equal partners.

I learned that day in October that one's appearance in the world of business can definitely make a difference. I learned how 20-somethings with body piercings and streaked hair can be discounted simply because they're not wearing the "corporate suit." The people who came up to me after our presentation asked us to keep sending out the message that great ideas, creativity, and know-how can come from employees in what appears to some to be strange packaging. As for myself, I have to say that flip-flops are truly comfortable.

Robin:

We all grew up hearing "don't judge a book by its cover," but also "dress to impress" and "your first impression will last forever." If you met me growing up, you'd have seen me as very trendy and even odd. When I entered the business world, I threw away my Madonna and Cindi Lauper clothes and switched to blue and gray conservative business suits.

Fortunately, styles have become a little more casual and fun these days. But looking young for my age and hearing "I have underwear older than you" or "how could you know anything, you're younger than my daughter," I've learned you have to dress extremely professionally and conform, or you won't gain respect for having any credibility or expertise. So you won't catch me wearing my flip-flops at a presentation, but I'll still keep them for the trip to my mailbox or grocery store where I have a chance to be sure I don't match.

Case Study: Interviewing Younger Generations

Imagine this common scenario if you will: an office with an interviewer/manager and an applicant for a position as assistant marketing director.

The director of marketing, the interviewer, is dressed in very conservative clothes, but is welcoming and cheerful. The young applicant is dressed in "hip" clothes and has a sharp notebook with her, in which she has a list of questions.

Let's call the interviewer "Linda" and the applicant "Robin."

Linda: Come in, Robin! Welcome to World Class Consulting. Please have a seat. [*motions to a seat that's across the desk/table and is lower than the one she's sitting in*]

Robin: Hi! [*takes a seat, but not before moving it to the side of the desk/table*)

Linda: I've been looking forward to meeting you. Our HR rep had some very nice things to say about your background, and I'm eager to fill the position of my assistant director. I've been the director for eight years now, and it's very fulfilling. We have a wonderful, enthusiastic team in our department and we contribute immensely to the organization. [*using her cheerleader voice*]

Robin: Thank you. I've been looking forward to learning more about whether my skills and education are a good fit for your company's culture.

Linda: Well, let me share some thoughts about this company's culture. We work very hard here, and we play hard when the work is accomplished. Because the industry we work in is fast-paced, our marketing team has to be cutting-edge to keep the company one step ahead of the competition. And we've successfully done that for several years.

Robin: Can you define "successful"? I didn't see any information on the company's Website about profitability and the organization's vision for the next five years with regard to market share.

Linda: I'd be happy to share all that later, but right now I'd like to find out more about *you* and your background. I see from your resume that you have a graduate degree from The University of Cincinnati....

Robin: Yes, I do. However, before we delve into my background, I really do want to know more about this organization's business plan and how the marketing department plans to support that plan. This will help me to understand whether your mission resonates with my personal wishes for the type of company where I want to work.

Linda: [*clearly exasperated*] Robin, I like to guide the interview process in a way that gets results for both of us, and I promise I'll include a discussion about our planning process *after* I learn some more about you and your background.

Robin: Can you at least tell me whether the assistant marketing director has a direct impact on the department's strategic plan? Does this person participate in the department and company strategic planning process?

Linda: Oh, I assure you that this position is an important part of our team. As the director, I lead the strategic planning process for the department and I attend, as our departmental representative, all corporate planning sessions. Now, as we were starting to discuss…what were your favorite courses at U.C. and why?

Robin: [*stands up*] I can see that this is not the position or company for me. I don't believe it's necessary to go any further. Thanks for your time. [*walks away, leaving Linda sitting open-mouthed at her desk*]

Questions for Discussion

1. Are there any generational mindsets that may be operating in this scenario?

2. How could the interviewer have conducted a more positive interview, resulting in Robin being interested and excited about the opening?

Solution

Robin is very likely a member of Generation Y, because she is friendly but not deferential towards her interviewer, a potential boss. She is casual in her demeanor and even takes it upon herself to rearrange Linda's interviewing set-up by moving a chair. Robin is intent upon finding out whether the company has core values that resonate with her own. Linda, on the other hand, may be a Baby Boomer or even a Radio Baby. She's dressed conservatively and has a "tried and true" interview method that she doesn't want disrupted. Linda is focused on finding out whether the candidate is right for the "team," whereas Robin is focused on finding out whether the company suits her needs.

Linda didn't frame the interview in a way that would allow for an open-ended dialogue, so she didn't have an opportunity to discover whether Robin was a suitable candidate. She could have set a more casual but still businesslike tone by conducting the interview at a round table, beside the candidate near her desk, or in a neutral conference room. If Linda wanted to understand Robin's work ethic and what type of activities stimulate her to be productive, she could have led with a description of some "hot" projects the company has successfully produced in the recent past. She could have observed Robin's reaction and comments to see whether these activities generated some interest. Unless a candidate asks for information about the company that is strictly proprietary, there is no reason not to share some highlights. In this case, the highlights could have been summarized on the company's Website so that candidates such as Robin could read about the company prior to setting up an interview.

An interview should be a "give and take" process—not an opportunity for interviewers to drill applicants. Linda could have been more flexible around the questions she asked and let Robin interject some questions of her own, making the process more collegial rather than "boss" and "subordinate." The message Linda telegraphed to Robin is, "This company, and myself in particular, is not open to challenge from younger employees."

Chapter 16

Frequently Asked Questions

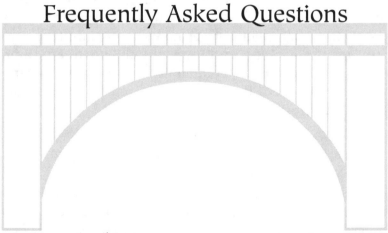

Linda and Robin:

Over the course of the last few years, we've observed a pattern in the types of questions we receive during speaking engagements and workshops. We'd like to share some of those frequently asked questions in this chapter and our response to each.

*How do you keep workers in their late 50s and early
60s from retiring?*

In a word: flexibility. This is a segment of the workforce
that is ready to phase into retirement and has less desire
to devote long, stressful hours to the workplace. However,
if your company can provide options such as telecommuting
opportunities, flexible hours, and job-sharing, you'll have a
higher likelihood of enticing this group of workers to stay a
while longer.

*Do Gen Ys have one-second attention spans? How
do you get and keep their attention?*

Because of the fast-paced, high-tech world in which
they grew up, many Ys do require a great deal of mental
stimulation and find it challenging to focus. In the workplace, we need to provide stimulating tasks and the best
technology we can afford to maintain this generation's interest. If we can demonstrate how our organization con-
tributes to society and how much we need them
individually to achieve community outreach, our organizations will have a better chance of getting and keeping
Gen Y's interest.

*Some of our older workers seem to just be riding out
their time until retirement. How do we get them engaged in their jobs?*

Put them to the task! Both Radio Babies and Baby
Boomers told us their brains still work, and they're going
to be around a long time. They like to share what they do
and why they do it. Give them the responsibility to mentor others and put their expertise and experiences to work
to help solve a problem or improve the company in a specific area. If that doesn't work, ask them what lights a fire
for them and engage them to make it happen.

Our company can't afford the latest "bells and whistles" and high starting salaries. How do we compete today for workers in any of the generations?

Some of the coveted concierge services that are available through organizations such as dry cleaners, automotive care companies, and personal shoppers, are available at no cost to employers. The vendors are happy to take care of the logistics, such as pickup of dirty laundry, if the company simply makes the service available. Conduct an employee survey first to discover what types of services your employees would like. Then let your fingers do the walking in the phone book or Internet yellow pages!

Are Baby Boomers and Gen Ys so far apart in terms of work ethic that they can't ever successfully work together?

Both generations want to work for profitable, successful organizations and receive recognition for a job well done. The only real difference between the two generations is the process of achieving results. Baby Boomers are more likely to believe long hours, office face-time, and receptivity to any offer for upward mobility are musts for career success. Gen Ys believe results-orientation, working smarter (not harder), and balancing work with personal life are critical to career success. If more Boomers would be open to learning how to use technology and current leadership techniques, they may be able to achieve results in less time (and less time behind their desk in the workplace). If Gen Ys would be open to learning more foundation skills before they can move into top positions, they may find that older colleagues are eager to help them succeed.

What if our customers and clients expect our staff to be professionally dressed—in a suit and tie or nice dress? How can we get that across to younger employees?

If your workforce interacts frequently with customers, make this fact known during the interview process. If a potential employee comes to the interview dressed too casually for your workplace, make sure to inform him or her that this is a requirement. Go to the next step, though, and let the candidate know *why* this is important, rather than saying, "Just do it." Also, consider giving new hires three to six months to build their wardrobe before strictly enforcing your dress code.

Why do older workers feel that they have to be everyone's parent?!

Many members of the Radio Baby generation spent their early years during very difficult times in the United States, economically speaking. If they were older siblings, they were likely to be called upon to take care of their younger brothers and sisters. Baby Boomers are members of larger families than previous generations. They too were often helping out with childcare, if for different reasons than Radio Babies. It's difficult for some to get past this when they start working with an increasingly younger workforce. Their children are the same age as new employees! If younger employees will assertively, respectfully share their ideas and the reasoning behind their perspectives, it will be easier for older coworkers to accept them as fully adult, participating members of the workforce.

How do you get a Gen Y to even show up to work?

If getting a Gen Y to show up to work is tough for your organization, you may have to do more than just make an offer to them. Remember that this is the generation that is compelled to join an organization by money, a friendly and casual work environment, and growth and development opportunities. Promising this during the interview isn't enough. Depending on the position, you could tie a bonus to working a week, a month, and/or a year. Likewise, you may want to continue reaching out to them after the offer has been extended and accepted by assigning a mentor to follow up before their start date, to give them an early taste of the office (such as a simple card signed by everyone welcoming them, a Starbucks gift card, or a Blockbuster gift card). Anything you can think of that will make them feel welcome, valued, and eager to join the team.

What is the biggest difference you have observed in the management style of Gen Xers and Baby Boomers?

We've observed that Boomers tend to hover more and be more hands-on, especially with new and/or younger direct reports. In *The Situational Leader*, Paul Hersey describes employees as either those who require specific direction or those who need only coaching, depending on the stage of their career and their individual level of sophistication. The Boomer managers, according to the Gen Ys and Gen Xers we interviewed, are too directive for too long with new employees. In other words, they tend to parent instead of providing the gentle coaching younger employees prefer. The Gen X managers we interviewed, however, prefer to be in the background and only be directly involved at the beginning of projects to communicate what results are expected. Then, Xer managers are more likely to step away and let direct reports come to them when they require assistance or have a question.

How do we help address the expectations of the younger generations coming into the workforce?

We found the dilemma about students' expectations and behavior to be a real issue, particularly in the last couple of years. We recommend employers consider working with schools to sponsor a class on entering the professional workforce in the high school curriculum. The class could address topics such as expectations in a professional workplace, use of company telephones and computers, and ethical behavior in the workplace. The class could have guest speakers (HR professionals, for example) from the industry, so the students don't think, "This is only the teacher's viewpoint."

Employers should also consider assigning a mentor to each incoming employee (interns and co-ops as well), someone who could "show them the ropes" and reiterate professional behavior standards. A thorough orientation should be provided to the students, addressing expectations regarding use of personal e-mail, phone calls, and so on. Department managers for whom the students work should be advised of these expectations and encouraged to (consistently) enforce the expectations.

What is the biggest source of conflict across generations in today's workplace?

By far the biggest "bone of contention" is philosophy of work ethic. Radio Babies and Boomers are more likely to expect employees (including themselves) to acquiesce to the organization's existing policies on work hours, benefits, and retirement. Gen X and Gen Y employees will question existing policies in order to understand why they're in place and why they must rigidly be applied. Boomers and Radio Babies more often identify work ethic as willingness to do things you don't want to do in order to advance one's career; Xers and Ys are more likely to characterize work ethic as ability to produce results.

Do Gen Ys feel a need to impress "the boss" in order to get ahead in their career?

No. Actually, Gen Ys are more likely to believe the boss should impress *them* in order to keep them content and to stay with the company. The Ys in our research are bold, confident, and certain of their capabilities, and therefore don't feel an overwhelming need to go out of their way to impress the boss. They're more likely to feel peer pressure within their own age group.

What do you think is the biggest hurdle to overcome to bridge the gap across generations?

We believe that eliminating negative (and false) stereotypes will be necessary in order to bridge the communications gap across generations. Though there are certainly some commonalities within the generations related to the times in which they grew up, individuals within each generation should be viewed as just that—individuals. We need to get past notions such as *all* 65-year-olds want to retire, or *all* 20-year-olds are tattooed and pierced.

Case Study: Managing Conflict With Younger Generations

Mary is a summer intern, working as a computer programmer for a high-tech services firm located in the Midwest. She's 20, and a junior at an Ivy League college. She'd rather be goofing off for the summer, but her father insisted that she work to get her first "real world" business experience. Mary's supervisor is Gordon, a 40-year-old who holds the position of IT manager. Gordon just started working for the company so he really wants to make a strong, positive impression. Most of his six-person team has a strong work ethic and, as he does, work long hours and take their jobs seriously. Mary, however, is a real concern. She seems more interested in hanging out in the staff's cubicles and talking programming theory than actually doing her work. Mary's job description entails low-level programming, preparing snail mail for IT staff, and getting lunch and the occasional dinner for staff when they're working late. Mary came into Gordon's office this morning, unannounced and without an appointment, and declared that the IT staff "yelled at her" when she didn't meet deadlines exactly on time; customers on the phone were rude and asked questions she didn't know the answer to; and she didn't want to get peoples' lunch or dinner because that's menial work. When Gordon said he'd have to think about how to respond to her "demands," she flounced out of his office and has been sulking at her desk ever since.

Questions for Discussion

1. Do you believe Mary's complaints are legitimate? Why or why not?

2. How, and when, should Gordon approach Mary to turn this situation around?

Solution

Mary was raised in a generation that received frequent praise and positive feedback. Mary is clearly more comfortable with being friends with her peers and even management staff, rather than considering them as on a different level than herself. She believes she has perfectly legitimate issues, based on her experiences at home and in school. If coworkers are truly being disrespectful to her, this is a valid concern that should be explored and addressed. Customers can indeed be rude, and that behavior can be influenced but certainly not controlled. No one wants to do menial, mindless work—or at least not all the time. Mary's generation is just more likely to speak up and speak out against it!

Gordon should approach Mary immediately to discuss this situation and not allow "sulking" to bring down the rest of the staff. Insubordinate, rude behavior should not be tolerated by any employee, regardless of age. He must remember, however, not to project his upbringing and experiences onto Mary. She may not have the same "work ethic" as he does; however, she can be encouraged to be a productive, contributing member of the staff during her internship.

Mary's job is what it is: entry level. That doesn't mean, however, that more interesting assignments cannot be interspersed into the more mundane tasks that Mary is required to complete. Perhaps she could "shadow" a more senior employee and provide assistance to him or her. When she does complete tasks such as picking up coworkers' lunch, Gordon (and the staff for whom she gets lunch) should thank her and show appreciation for her effort.

Many employees in Mary's generation need skill-building in the area of customer service and dealing with conflict. Part of the orientation could include these topics, not just for younger employees but for any incoming employee.

As to the allegation that coworkers "yell" at her, Gordon will need to explore this issue further. Mary may be characterizing coworkers exhibiting frustration or stress as "yelling," when indeed they don't even raise their voice to her. Teaching younger employees how to increase their emotional intelligence—in the way they interact with others—is an excellent investment that will result in less conflict and more productive approaches.

Research Results

Interview/Survey Time Frame: 2000–2002
(Follow-up interviews conducted in late 2004 and early 2005)

Interviewees: 500 people in each of four age groups:

AGE	GENERATION
58–73	Radio Babies
39–57	Baby Boomers
27–38	Generation X
18–26	Generation Y

Questions

1. What factors affect your happiness in general?
2. What entices you (or would entice you) to join an organization?
3. What compels you to stay with a company?
4. What factors shaped your perspectives when you were growing up?
5. What characteristics of other generations in the workplace bother you the most?
6. What do you want other generations to know about you and your generation?

NOTE: Some respondents gave multiple answers to a given question or declined to answer at all.

1. What factors affect your happiness in general?

	#	%
Radio Babies		
❏ Feeling of financial security	239	52
❏ Personal or spouse's health	103	22
❏ Family's happiness	87	19
❏ Economic conditions	23	5
❏ World events/feeling of safety	8	2

Baby Boomers

❏ Feeling of financial security	196	40
❏ Job or community status	167	34
❏ Political arena	98	20
❏ Family's happiness	19	4
❏ Personal or spouse's health	12	2

Generation X

❏ Family's happiness	202	44
❏ World events/feeling of safety	113	24
❏ Leisure time availability/quality	107	23
❏ Political arena (local level)	30	7
❏ Happiness with job	10	2

Generation Y

❏ Friendships (quality)	163	33
❏ School involvement/activities	120	24
❏ Happiness with job	107	21
❏ World events/feeling of safety	90	18
❏ Community/political involvement	20	4

2. What entices you (or would entice you) to join an organization?

	#	%
Radio Babies		
❏ Flexible, tailored benefits	238	49
❏ Job security	192	39
❏ Opportunity to use experience	60	12

Baby Boomers

- ❏ Salary, title, status   197   45
- ❏ Flexible, tailored benefits   130   29
- ❏ Learning opportunities/challenges 113   26

Generation X

- ❏ Match between company and
personal values   173   43
- ❏ Salary and benefits package   118   29
- ❏ Growth opportunities   115   28

Generation Y

- ❏ Salary   189   50
- ❏ Friendly, casual work environment 105   27
- ❏ Growth opportunities   87   23

3. What compels you to stay with a company?

	#	%

Radio Babies

- ❏ Experience/expertise is respected 157   38
- ❏ Flexible, tailored benefits   138   33
- ❏ Company shows loyalty   123   29

Baby Boomers

- ❏ Advancement opportunities   115   38
- ❏ Experience/expertise is respected 102   33
- ❏ Work continues to be interesting   90   29

Generation X

- ❏ Career development opportunities 207   44
- ❏ Ability to enjoy work–life balance   176   37
- ❏ Company has values/integrity   87   19

Generation Y

- ❏ Ideas/input valued and respected 183   47
- ❏ Career development opportunities 118   30
- ❏ Quality service or product   91   23

4. What factors shaped your perspectives when you were growing up?

	#	%
Radio Babies		
❏ Parents' views	147	45
❏ Community values	103	31
❏ Respected leaders	77	24
Baby Boomers		
❏ Family views	139	42
❏ Friends' values and views	99	30
❏ Political events (Civil Rights)	94	28
Generation X		
❏ World events as seen on TV	163	43
❏ Friends' values and views	137	36
❏ A handful of respected coworkers	80	21

Generation Y
- ❏ Community values and lifestyles   158   51
- ❏ Grandparents' views   83   27
- ❏ World events as seen on TV   67   22

5. What characteristics of other generations in the workplace bother you the most?

	#	%

Radio Babies
- ❏ People in their early 20s
  don't respect their elders   197   44
- ❏ People in their early 20s
  have no work ethic   180   40
- ❏ Young people are impatient
  for career success   74   16

Baby Boomers
- ❏ Young people have no loyalty
  to the company   182   52
- ❏ People in their 20s and 30s
  have no work ethic   107   31
- ❏ Young people are impatient
  for career success   61   17

Generation X
- ❏ Baby Boomers are too bossy   176   46
- ❏ Radio Babies won't accept change   118   30
- ❏ People in their teens and early 20s
  have no work ethic   93   24

Generation Y

	#	%
❏ Older employees are bossy and set in their ways	170	44
❏ Older people don't understand technology	127	33
❏ Older people don't treat me with respect	88	23

6. What do you want other generations to know about you and your generation?

	#	%
Radio Babies		
❏ My brain is still functioning	207	47
❏ There are good reasons to do things certain ways	164	37
❏ I want to continue to work	70	16
Baby Boomers		
❏ I'll be around for a long time	183	48
❏ I'm not an aging hippie	117	30
❏ There are good reasons to do things certain ways	84	22
Generation X		
❏ I have made/can make contributions to society	164	48
❏ I will not stay in a company that has no integrity	97	28
❏ I have a good work ethic	80	24

Generation Y

❏ I want to make a difference   173   54

❏ I expect to be treated with respect 84   26
❏ I won't play by your rules
    without a good reason   63   20

Worksheet:
Calculating Turnover Costs

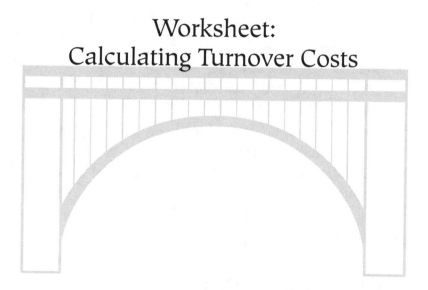

Turnover Ratio: The number of employees who left, divided by the average number of people employed per year.

Separation Costs

1. Interviewer's Time (hours spent × hourly rate*) $_____
2. Terminated Employee's Time
   (while on payroll: hours spent × hourly rate) $_____
3. HR Administrative Functions
   (termination paperwork:
   hours spent × hourly rate) $_____
4. Separation Pay $_____

Total Separation Costs $_____

*include benefits in the hourly rate

Replacement Costs

1. Advertising $_____
2. Internal Communications
   (development time × hourly rate) $_____
3. Interview Time
   (hours spent × hourly rate for interviewer) $_____
4. Administrative Functions
   (typing, copying: hours spent × hourly rate) $_____
5. Applicant Testing
   (such as validated aptitude tests) $_____
6. Applicant Travel Expenses $_____
7. Applicant Relocation Expenses $_____

Total Replacement Costs $_____

Training Costs

1. Employee workbooks
   (printing + time for development × hourly rate) $_____

2. Orientation(s)
   (new employee time + staff time × hourly rates) $_____
3. On-the-job training
   (employees' time × hourly rates) $_____

Total Training Costs $_____

Separation + Replacement + Training $____

Per Employee Cost

(total costs ÷ number left in the company) $_____

Appendix C

Generation Birth-Years

Radio Babies:	1930–1945
Baby Boomers:	1946–1964
Generation X:	1965–1976
Generation Y:	1977–1990
Millennials:	1991 and later

Reference List

Bailey, Chris. 2002. Why care about Generation Y?
www.hr.state.tx.us/features/article.html/item/8

Brokaw, Tom. 2001. *The Greatest Generation.* New York:
Random House, Inc.

Bureau of Labor Statistics. www.bls.gov

Dohm, Arlene. 2000. Gauging the labor force effects of retiring baby-boomers. www.bls.gov/opub/mlr/2000/07/art2exc.htm

Equal Employment Opportunity Commission. www.ucsf.edu/wrklife/wlrc_newsletter.htm

Farren, Caela. 2003. Generation Y: A new breed of values and desires. *MasteryWorks, Inc.* www.masteryworks.com

Goldberg, Beverly. 2003. *Age Works.* New York: The Free Press.

Grossman, Robert. 2003. Are you ignoring older workers? *HR Magazine.* August 1: 41–46.

Hacker, Carol. 2003. Recruiting and retaining 'Generation Y and X' employees. *PMQ Magazine.* www.chartcourse.com/articlegenxhacker.html

Hersey, Paul. 1997. *The Situational Leader.* Escondido: Center for Leadership Studies. www.chimaeraconsulting.com/sitleader.htm

Howe, Neil and William Strauss. 2000. *Millennials Rising.* New York: Vintage Books. www.millennialsrising.com

Knable, Thomas. 2001. Why are baby boomers returning to college? adulted.about.com/library/weekly/aa021901a.htm

Kudlow, Lawrence. 2005. Kudlow's money politic$. *Wall Street Journal.* December 12, 2005.

L'Allier, James, Ph.D., and Kenneth Kolosh, 2005. Preparing for Baby Boomer retirement. *Chief Learning Officer.* www.clomedia.com/content/templates/clo_article.asp?articleid=976

Lenhart, Amanda, Mary Madden, and Paul Hitlin. 2005. Washington, D.C.: Pew Internet & American Life Project. www.pewinternet.org/pdfs/ PIP_teens_tech_july2005web.pdf

Massey, Morris. 1979. *The People Puzzle*. Englewood Cliffs: Reston Publishing.

McCaleb, Ian Christopher. 2000. Overshadowed generation prepares to steer political agenda, author claims. archives.cnn.com/2000/ALLPOLITICS/stories/ 03/05/generation.jones/index.html

Muson, Howard. 2003. Valuing experience: how to motivate and retain mature workers. The Conference Board, #R-1329-03-RR. www.conference-board.org

Pierce, Linda Green. 2006. Gen X change the rules. *North west Legal Search*. www.nwlegalsearch.com/articles/ generation_x.html

Raines, Claire. 2000. *Generations at Work*. New York: AMACOM.

Singhania, Lisa. 2002. Boomers shift outlook on work. *The Boston Globe*, 12/22/02: H2.

Smith, Gregory. 2005. Baby Boomer versus Generation X. *Recruiters Network*. www.chartcourse.com/ articlebabyvsgenx.html

Spherion Employment Report. 2005. Worker confidence and job market rebound in November. www.spherion.com/press/releases/2005/ november05_employee_rep.jsp

Stevens-Huffman, Leslie. 2005. Could your best hire be a 'recareering Boomer'? *Workforce Magazine*. www.workforce.com/archive/article/24/23/28.php

Tulgan, Bruce, and Dr. Carolyn Martin. 2002. Managing the generation mix—part II. www.rainmakerthinking.com/backwttw/2002/feb19.htm

Index

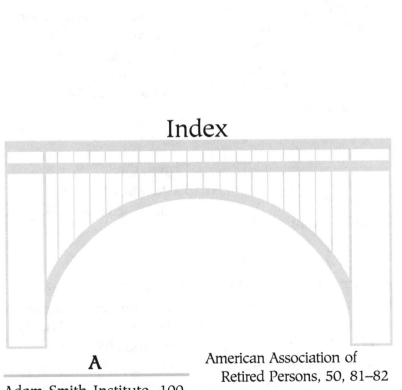

About the Authors

Linda S. Gravett, Ph.D., SPHR

Dr. Gravett is senior partner of Gravett and Associates, an organizational development consulting firm headquartered in Cincinnati, Ohio, and co-founder of e-HResources.com, an online consulting firm. She has consulted with organizations such as Dole, Williams-Sonoma, and Perfetti Van Melle over the past 15 years. Dr. Gravett is a frequent speaker at professional conferences on the topics of HRM ethics, leveraging workplace diversity, and gender and generational differences. She is the also the author of *HRM Ethics: Perspectives for a New Millennium*, published in 2002.

Robin Throckmorton, M.A., SPHR

Robin Throckmorton is the founder of and senior consultant with Strategic HR, Inc., a human resources management consulting firm headquartered in Cincinnati, Ohio, and co-founder of e-HResources.com, an online consulting firm. She has been a consultant for more than 10 years with healthcare, manufacturing, service, and non-profit organizations, creating solutions to help them recruit and retain the best and the brightest employees. Robin is a frequent speaker for professional associations and conferences on the topics of generational differences, retention, recruitment strategies, and labor trends.